GRANDBABY CAKES

GRANDBABY
CAKES

Modern Recipes • Vintage Charm • Soulful Memories

~ Jocelyn Delk Adams ~

S
SURREY
BOOKS

AN **AGATE** IMPRINT

CHICAGO

Food photography copyright by Jocelyn Delk Adams
Family portraits and photography copyright by Chuck Olu-Alabi
Wedding photography copyright by James Rubio
Food styling by Jesse Szewczyk
Art direction/prop styling by Leslie Watland

Printed in China

Library of Congress Cataloging-in-Publication Data

Adams, Jocelyn Delk.
  Grandbaby cakes : modern recipes, vintage charm, soulful memories / Jocelyn Delk Adams ; photography by Jocelyn Delk Adams and Chuck Olu-Alabi.
    pages cm
  Includes index.
  "Cookbook featuring 50 vintage cakes with modern twists and memoir tracing the roots of
the author's family recipes"--Provided by publisher
  ISBN 978-1-57284-173-4 (hardback) -- ISBN 1-57284-173-7 (hard cover) -- ISBN 978-1-57284-
760-6 (ebook)
  1. Cake. I. Title.
  TX771.A327 2015
  641.86'53--dc23
          2015013216

Surrey Books is an imprint of Agate Publishing. Agate books can be purchased in bulk at
discount prices. Visit agatepublishing.com for more information.

10 9 8 7 6 5 4 3 2 1

*For my loving family who taught me that life's
lessons are best learned over dessert.*

*To my dear friend Leonore, thank you for being
a guardian angel in the kitchen with me.*

Contents

Pound Cakes

Layer Cakes

Sheet Cakes

Baby Cakes

Celebration Cakes

Seasons *and* Holidays

Foreword

Hootie hoo, good people! This is Carla Hall, and I sincerely believe in creating food that "hugs" you. When I was growing up in Tennessee, I learned a great deal about the true meaning of comfort food from my granny. Sunday suppers were more like *soul* suppers, consisting of a healthy dose of love, compassion, and wisdom (not to mention some of the best food I have ever tasted). I always looked forward to dessert, especially when Granny made her famous five-flavor pound cake. Her cakes always tasted like the type of warm, Southern hug that only a grandmother could properly give. Each bite was a morsel of sunshine, and each slice had the unique power of making any day better.

As I grew older, I realized the true gift food was in my life and how transformative it can be. I didn't fully appreciate all that Granny had to offer me in the way of cooking and baking techniques when I was young, but she instilled in me the life lesson of infusing every single thing I created with love. When the cooking-and-baking bug bit me at 25, all of a sudden I felt like I was playing catch-up. Granny was and will always be my inspiration.

Cooking from the heart is my motto, and there is no better way of expressing that than with comfort food. From a small country kitchen in Nashville to some of the most renowned kitchens in the world,

Cooking from the heart is my motto, and there is no better way of expressing that than with comfort food.

Granny's teachings have blessed and connected me with so many people from all walks of life. No matter what language you speak or what background you come from, the universal language of love can be felt and experienced by anyone, especially in food.

Speaking this language actually led me to meeting Jocelyn. I always say that the universe makes no mistakes, and that phrase couldn't have been any truer than when I received a tweet from Jocelyn out of the blue. All I saw were the words "Grandbaby Cakes" and a photo of Jocelyn's smiling face. For some reason, I felt compelled to connect with her, and I am so glad I did. I invited her to breakfast, and our similar personalities hit it off right away. It felt natural. She ended up showing me some images of a photo shoot she took with her grandmother for this cookbook. I realized that we not only shared a love of food, but we also cherished the bond of a grandmother's love. It reminded me of my sacred memories with Granny. It truly touched me, and from that moment on, Jocelyn and I became friends and kindred spirits.

When she asked me to write the foreword for her first cookbook, I was honored to do it. The love and tradition steeped in her recipes are clear influences from her grandmother and the rest of her family roots. But I can definitely see the playful touch and modern impact Jocelyn gives as well. This book is a tribute to those who know where they came from and also where they are going. Each cake is baked with the same love I grew up knowing and experiencing during my younger days back in Nashville. They are trips down memory lane that end with delicious treats on your table.

No matter what language you speak or what background you come from, the universal language of love can be felt and experienced by anyone, especially in food.

Introduction

Big Daddy, my mom, Big Mama, and Uncle Sidney

"YOU CAN'T KNOW WHERE YOU'RE GOING UNTIL YOU KNOW WHERE you've been." This age-old saying couldn't be more appropriate for describing the life journey that ultimately led to me writing this book. When I was young, my family routinely embarked on a 10-hour journey from our hometown of Chicago to Winona, Mississippi, to visit my maternal grandparents, Sid and Maggie Small. Now, at the age of 34, I can say that this tradition has not ceased.

My grandmother, whom we affectionately call Big Mama, always took pleasure in creating a gorgeous centerpiece cake. Sometimes she would wait until we arrived, and the women would roll up their sleeves and head into the kitchen for baking and catching up. I treasured these moments when my Big Mama, mom, and auntie would let me dabble in the process as a rite of passage. They were never fazed by my ceaseless curiosity and countless questions in the midst of their magic

making. I especially loved when it was time to sift the flour, and I would stare in awe as it fell like delicate snow into the mixing bowl.

Big Mama never required a timer; just a whiff of a baked good's fragrance in the air was enough for her to know it was ready. While the baking pan was piping hot, she would slide it out of the oven and onto the grates of the stove. The anticipation was always brutal—I could not wait to tear into the steaming temptation before me. Finally, Big Mama would take pity on her impatient grandbaby and hand me a fork. She didn't mind if I snuck a bite or two, because she'd made the cake for me anyway. And I didn't mind sneaking a small sliver to my Big Daddy, who has an insatiable sweet tooth. He would giggle and thank his grandbaby before slyly whispering to me to not tell my grandmother.

I have been a dessert lover for as long as I can remember (starting with my early Easy Bake Oven creations), and Big Mama's cakes are the best I ever tasted. They are rich in flavor, and the crumb is so moist it literally melts in my mouth. From tree-picked fruit to farm-raised chicken eggs and fresh-churned butter (thanks to Big Mama's cow, Betsy), Big Mama first began using these gifts to build her dessert monuments with billowing buttercream adorning her creations. These cakes are works of art.

My childhood recollections are rich and deep, brimming with nostalgia for Big Mama's freshly baked cakes. Watching my family make these recipes—and learning how to make them myself—taught me patience (anything worth having should never be rushed), forgiveness (sometimes things don't always turn out perfectly, but that's OK), selflessness (giving of yourself is the best gift you can ever give), and love (the most important ingredient you can ever add to your cakes). The life lessons I learned in Big Mama's kitchen forever shaped my character. Stories about how her mother died when she was a young girl, how she invented all the recipes that were passed down to me, the fun she had ringing the supper bell to assemble her daddy and 13 siblings from working in the fields all day for dinner, her long days at working at the local hospital, and the crazy things my mom, uncles, and aunt did that got them into trouble back in the day are etched in my memory.

Big Mama's recipe techniques are humble, but so sophisticated in flavor and influence. Her cakes are the love notes of my family, the fabric of our heritage. They

Ed Thomas, Big Mama's father

*Big Mama and fellow nursing assistants at
Memorial Hospital in Winona, Mississippi*

were called upon for every history-making event, from a church picnic and minister dinner to a wedding or a college graduation. I hope to honor them, and the men and women in my family who unknowingly shaped me into the fearless, confident, loving, driven woman I am through the decades of lessons learned in the kitchen. Back then, the kitchen was our place of refuge and transformed into everything from a Sunday church service beauty parlor (for pressing hair) to a family therapy session hub.

The echoes of these memories were the genesis of my website, Grandbaby Cakes. My tagline, "Vintage Recipes, Fresh Twists, Soulful Memories" sums it up perfectly. It was only fitting that a cookbook of eclectic bold new cake recipes with the heart and soul of my past would follow. This collection isn't meant to supply you with only run-of-the-mill yellow cakes and plain Bundt cake recipes. Most of us already have more than enough of those old family heirlooms to choose from. Instead, the Grandbaby Cakes book will offer you a few must-have classics paired alongside a variety of fun and hip cake creations with exciting new flavors for you to explore. Baking is all about chemistry and magic, and I hope these recipes will fill you with the same sense of adventure and excitement I had while developing them. I also hope it inspires you to reconnect and delve deep into your own generational family history to relive the tales of your unique heritage. We all have these priceless stories lurking in our past. We just need to commit to digging them up and passing them along. In fact, I invite you to write to me anytime at gbcakesbook@gmail.com to tell me if this book has impacted you in any way.

I wrote this book with new-aged bakers who crave a little of their roots in mind. Every single cake recipe was tested by a baker just like you. Ranging from expert bakers to beginners, they sent me tons of advice to make these recipes work for you in the best way possible. Remember, you don't have to fit the stereotype of a "traditional" baker. I certainly don't. My lifestyle is more in line with a big-city hipster with a fast-paced career than the life of my grandmother's, but I am at my most inspired in the kitchen. And you can be too! In my world, I'd rather welcome the new neighbors with a homemade pound cake than a bottle of wine—especially if it's a Pineapple Upside-Down Hummingbird Pound Cake (p. 53). Talk about making an impression!

Cake is always a charming gift or addition to a potluck, a great nod to tradition and Southern hospitality with a bit of contemporary flair and heart. Don't be intimidated to roll up your sleeves and get a little dirty. Add a family member to help, and the results will be more fun than you have had in years. Just remember that in spite of everything, anything baked with love will always get applause.

How to Use This Book

THIS BOOK IS THE BAKING BOOK FOR YOU IF:

- ☞ You are an experienced baker looking to turn up the volume on some classics, but you still want to maintain the nostalgia of traditional recipes,

- ☞ You are intimidated by baking and want to start small by building yourself up to more advanced scratch cake recipes, or

- ☞ You love cakes! And I mean moist, delicious, can't-put-your-fork-down, eat-every-last-crumb, unforgettable cakes.

If any of these describe you, then you are in the right place!

Levels

Each recipe in this book is broken down by the following classifications to give you an idea of the time commitment, steps, and effort needed to create the cake:

 Grandbaby Cakes usually require the least amount of time and effort, clocking in at less than an hour for prep and baking. They are usually also the easiest to create! If you are a novice baker, this level should be your first stop.

 Mama Cakes are intermediate-level cakes that also require a bit more time. Most clock in at around one to three hours for prep and baking time. They demand a little more expertise and have more steps and ingredients. However, the additional effort pays off.

 Big Mama Cakes are the most advanced recipes in the book. They sometimes have more than three steps or components and may even require an overnight stage. Some demand additional equipment, like an ice cream maker or a butane torch. If you can get through the Grandbaby Cakes level with little effort, you should definitely take the plunge into this category. The rewards are worth it.

In most of the recipes you will also find tips, which I call "Grandbaby Notes." Please ensure that you read these before you begin baking. There are some great nuggets that apply to the specific recipes.

My Baking Rules

● USING A COMBINATION OF BUTTER AND OIL

A lot of my recipes combine the rich flavor of butter with the moistness of vegetable oil. Nowadays I don't like to choose one over the other because they both have undeniable benefits. To me, using both is the best of both worlds. However, if I must select just one, I choose oil for cakes that don't require the rich, creamy flavor butter provides. My chocolate cake recipes, like the Mississippi Mudslide Cake (p. 77), are great examples of this. The chocolate should be the "Batman," so the oil slides right in like Robin, taking a backseat to the chocolate's intensity, only yielding moistness as needed. However, in my pound cake recipes, butter is crucial to the overall flavor of the finished product.

● NO STICKING AROUND THESE PARTS!

For the majority of my baking, I use a good-quality nonstick baking spray. You can easily find this at your local grocery store in the cooking oil or baking sections. I love it because it is so convenient. My pans are good and worn in, so a solid coating of spray does the trick. However, my Big Mama and mom subscribe to the shortening-and-flour trick (like the one described below). It may be a bit more tedious, but nothing sticks with it.

It really depends on your pans. I want you to get to know them and their moods, so to speak. If they have a tendency to stick, you will need more heft than the baking spray will provide. For layer cakes, I usually spray the pan, line the bottom with parchment paper, and then also spray the paper to ensure that everything pops out perfectly.

If you have time, I recommend creating your own nonstick solution as follows: one part oil, one part shortening, and one part all-purpose flour mixed together and brushed on baking pans. The results are incredible. Nothing is sticking to your pans with that baby! Can I get an AMEN?

● SIFTING

Big Mama sifts flour for every single cake she bakes. I, on the other hand, skip this step a lot if I am running out of time—but I always sift if I am baking for other people. I definitely recommend sifting flour for the recipes in this book. It lightens a cake like none other. However, if you don't sift the flour, you will still have quite a delicious cake in the end. Trust me.

CREAMING

I know there are millions of new cake-mixing techniques, and some are absolutely grand, but I tend to stick to the traditional method of creaming. Creaming is simply mixing your fat and sugar together to incorporate as much air into your baked good as possible. Some of the cakes in this book do not use a chemical leavening agent (like your standard baking powder or baking soda), so this step is very crucial. By whipping in as much air as possible, you will get that lovely rise you need.

FROSTING YOUR CAKE

Several of the layer cakes in this book require frosting. The best tools for a really clean look are an offset spatula and a bench scraper. If you want to take it one step further, invest in a cake turntable. It makes frosting cakes so much easier.

BASIC FROSTING INSTRUCTIONS

Make sure the cake layers are completely cooled. I like to refrigerate my layers for at least 30 minutes before frosting for two reasons: It prevents me from having to do a crumb coat (a quick base coat of frosting to seal in crumbs—crumbs easily tear from cake layers when a cake is at room temperature), and it firms up the layers, making them easier to stack and work with overall.

Place one layer on a turntable or serving plate lined with parchment paper strips on the edge of the cake.

Add a large dollop of frosting to the center of the first layer. Using your offset spatula, spread the frosting evenly over the surface of the layer (not the sides). Carefully push from the center out to the edge.

Once the bottom layer is completely frosted, gently place the second cake layer on top. Repeat the frosting process.

Add the third layer bottom-side up (meaning the flat bottom of the cake should be facing up). Add a large amount of frosting to the center of the top layer and spread over the top, pushing toward the edge and down the side of the cake. The frosting will naturally begin to fall over the side, which is what you want to happen.

Continue to go around the side of the cake, adding more frosting if needed, making sure everything is covered. Let the spatula do its handy work. At this point, if you want a clean finish, you can use a bench scraper and carefully go around the cake and gather up extra frosting; however, I like a homemade cake to look very homemade, so I love the rustic unfinished look of extra frosting.

● STORING YOUR CAKE

Most cakes, whether frosted or unfrosted, are usually just fine stored at room temperature. Growing up, we used a domed cake plate to store a cake on the counter for up to four days until it was consumed. This went for frosted cakes and pound cakes. Frosted cakes have the luxury of a buttercream barrier that helps to keep them moist and fresh. However, any cakes with whipped cream or cream cheese buttercreams should always be stored in the refrigerator. Those last up to three days.

● FREEZING YOUR LAYER CAKE

During the testing of this book, I froze many of the layer cakes to preserve them for photo shoots and family tastings. You won't believe how fresh the cakes can taste if you just use my tips below.

- Thoroughly wrap each unfrosted layer in two sheets of plastic wrap immediately after it's placed on a wire rack, making sure every inch is completely covered.
- Next, add each separate layer to a resealable plastic bag and close tightly. Make sure you have released all of the air from the bag before closing.
- Label the cake with its type and the freeze date. Then transfer to the freezer, laying each layer completely flat.
- When ready to serve, just allow your layers to come to room temperature and proceed with frosting them or finishing the presentation.

Ingredients

You can find the majority of ingredients for these recipes from your local grocery store. No need to get too fussy if you don't want to. However, there are a few items that you may need to source. Below I share all you need to know to get started.

● BUTTER

There is no denying that butter can truly make the difference in the flavor of a cake, and you haven't lived until you've tasted a cake made with a high-fat-content butter. Most American butters found in your grocery store have around 80 percent fat content, but with European butter, the butterfat content starts around 82 percent and can go as high as 88 percent, which decreases the amount of water in the product. Just imagine all of that rich flavor baking into your cake. Unsalted butter brands like Plugrá and Kerrygold have 82 percent fat, which you can find at most grocery stores or your local high-end grocer. However, I tested all of these cakes with standard American butter like Land O'Lakes from my local grocery store, so I know that they taste fantastic with this type as well.

Most of my recipes will request you start with butter at room temperature. This basically means that your butter should be soft enough for your thumb to leave an indent when you lightly press. If the butter completely smushes under your thumb, it's too soft and you should put it back in your refrigerator to firm up some. It will not cream properly otherwise.

For recipes that call for melted butter, I just put a stick (eight tablespoons) in a microwave-safe bowl and heat for 20 to 30 seconds, watching every 5 to 10 seconds after until it is completely melted.

● UNSALTED VERSUS SALTED BUTTER

Pastry chefs are sure to raise an eyebrow when I say this, but I grew up on cakes made with salted butter. The cakes always tasted amazing, so to me, the butter used really makes no difference. I personally use unsalted in my baking and add salt separately because it gives me more control, but please don't believe that I would ever hesitate to use salted butter if a cake craving called and that was all I had in the fridge. If you like using salted, just omit any additional salt listed in the recipe.

● SHORTENING

A few of my recipes will call for a touch of vegetable shortening. I know using it can be a sore spot for some, but a pinch of it will moisten your cakes and won't do you any harm. Case in point, my Big Mama has been using it every day for decades, and both of my grandparents are in great health in their late 80s.

● CHOCOLATE

I use natural unsweetened cocoa powder (not Dutch processed) for the chocolate-based cakes in this book. You can readily find brands like Hershey's and Nestlé Toll House or higher-end brands like Ghirardelli and Valrhona in your grocery store. For these cakes, you can definitely use whatever you find. I also use bittersweet and semisweet chocolate in some recipes. Semisweet chocolate is a tiny bit sweeter than the deeper chocolaty bittersweet, but these two can be interchanged for the most part with no problems.

DAIRY

I don't use light milk in any of my batters. In my experience, the cakes come out a bit dryer, with more of a cornbread consistency, which is not exactly my idea of a cake. Instead, I love using full-fat sour cream, buttermilk, whole milk, and heavy cream. You can even use Greek yogurt as a great substitute for sour cream.

SWEETENED CONDENSED MILK VS. EVAPORATED MILK

Both milks will be called for in this book, however I want to point out some very key differences between the two. While both technically have had about 60 percent water removed, sweetened condensed milk adds 40 percent sugar. I like to think of sweetened condensed milk as sweetened evaporated milk and evaporated milk as unsweetened condensed milk. I hope I didn't confuse you too much. Basically, the moral of this tale is to never swap these ingredients. They are not interchangeable.

EGGS

I use only large eggs in my baking. They are the standard baking size and won't require any additional searching. To bring them to room temperature quickly, simply submerge them in a bowl of lukewarm water. They will be ready for baking in no time. For safety purposes, especially when baking for children, I always use pasteurized eggs like Safest Choice.

FLOURS

I mostly use cake flour in my recipes. It started out as a habit, because both Big Mama and my mother taught me to bake with it. However, I tested using both all-purpose and cake flours, and the majority of the time I preferred cake flour. There is a lightness and airiness, due to cake flour's lower protein percentage, that my cakes' texture benefits from. The results are soft and fine—just how I love a cake to be.

There are a few recipes that use all-purpose flour, however, because I wanted to add a stronger structure to the cake. In those instances, make sure you always purchase unbleached. Also, ensure that you don't exchange one flour for another, because the type of flour was hand-selected for each recipe. The results will surely be different if you don't use the ingredients as listed.

FOOD COLORING

The recipes in this book were tested with liquid food coloring because you can easily find it in your grocery store. However, you can always use gel or paste—just make sure that you proceed carefully and slowly. Only use a little to start, increasing the amount until you reach your desired color. Liquid food coloring gives the weakest color, requiring more drops to deepen the intensity; gel or paste food coloring provides very concentrated and vivid results, so a little can be used to supply the same outcome as liquid.

This is a very controversial topic for many home cooks who do not like using food coloring in their baking. There are now many wonderful natural food colorings on the market. I recently saw several red colorings made with beet juice at my neighborhood health food store. I think these natural colorings are great options for getting you the color you want in a manner you are comfortable with.

● FRUIT

There are several recipes in this book that use seasonal fruit. You can, of course, make substitutions when necessary. Just make sure that the fruit is the same texture, moisture, and structure as the original fruit. Simply put, stay in the same fruit family. For instance, I wouldn't suggest swapping berries for watermelon. Due to water content, anatomy, and even sweetness, you will get totally different results. If strawberries are called for, try using another berry, and taste as you go along so you can adjust other ingredients as you see fit.

● LEAVENINGS

Baking powder and baking soda can be found in the majority of recipes in this book. They help give the lift needed to make your cakes rise like a star. Playing with their amounts can be quite tricky if you don't know the science behind them. For the purposes of this book, just make sure that you keep fresh leavening on hand. Once it expires, your cake won't lift. Here are two simple ways to test the activation of your leavening: For baking soda, add ¼ teaspoon to 2 teaspoons of vinegar. If it bubbles instantly, it is good to go. For baking powder, add 1 teaspoon to ½ cup of hot water. If it fizzes immediately, it is good to go.

● SALT

This ingredient is more crucial to a well-balanced and flavorful cake than you will ever know. I don't tend to get too particular about salt type. If all you have is iodized table salt, so be it! Use it. My personal preference is finely ground sea salt, but I use whatever I have on hand to get the job done.

● SUGAR

The majority of the recipes in this book call for granulated or light brown sugar, both of which are readily available at most grocery stores. For most frostings, you will need confectioners' sugar, also known as powdered sugar.

● VANILLA EXTRACT AND OTHER FLAVORINGS

Pure flavorings can really bring a cake to life. From vanilla to fruit-flavored bases, you will find quite a few used in recipes throughout this book. Quality is key when selecting these products. Never use artificial flavorings. There are so many amazing options out there that you never have to go this route. Nielsen-Massey and LorAnn Oils are great brands. Their extracts and pastes are high quality, and the taste is always authentic and amazing. Boyajian has wonderful fruit-based oils that can take the place of zests. A little goes a long way, and the quality is fantastic. In addition to being able to order these online, you can also find them in fine stores like Williams-Sonoma and Sur La Table. For a great grocery store brand of extracts, I use McCormick.

● SPICES

There are several recipes that call for rich spices like cinnamon and nutmeg in the book. For special-occasion baking, I head to my local spice shop to pick up premium hand-prepared spices. However, you don't have to get too prissy in this department. Jarred spices from brands like McCormick are just as great for regular baking.

● CAKE BOX MIXES

Every recipe in this book can be made entirely scratch; however, there are a few shortcuts mentioned where cake mix can be used. Though I am a from-scratch type of gal, I have never stuck my nose up in the air over cake mix. Big Mama has certainly used some in her day. It has its place and provides a steady, reliable, and convenient solution in times of dessert trouble. My goal has always been to get people into the kitchen, so if you must start with a cake mix to get over any baking anxiety, so be it! However, I do want you to try your hand at the easier from-scratch recipes as well. Once you conquer one, you will be baking from scratch regularly in no time.

Best Baking Tools

BIG MAMA DEFINITELY HAD SOME OF THE BEST BAKEWARE AVAILABLE IN her heyday. From a classic Sunbeam mixer and reliable wooden spoons to floral patterned mixing bowls and a rock salt ice cream maker, she had the tools for great success in her kitchen. For the same success in life, or maybe just in baking, stock your kitchen with the following tools:

- 10-cup and 12-cup Bundt pans (There are some gorgeous varieties out there. Nordic Ware makes some lovely decorative pieces that will truly turn your pound cakes into masterpieces.)
- 10-inch round pan or cast-iron skillet
- two 12-well muffin pans
- two 5-cup, 6-well mini Bundt pans
- 2-quart ice cream maker
- four 6-ounce ramekins
- 4- or 5-quart stand mixer (I use KitchenAid)
- five 9-inch round cake pans
- 9 × 11-inch baking sheet
- 9 × 13-inch rectangular cake pan
- butane torch
- cake turntable, for frosting
- coffee stirrers, for testing cake readiness
- cupcake liners
- electronic kitchen scale, to exactly measure the amount of batter in each pan
- flour sifter
- food processor or heavy-duty blender, for fruit and veggie purées

- glass trifle bowl
- hand mixer (While I use a stand mixer for all of these recipes, you can easily replace that with a hand mixer and large bowl.)
- lightweight mixing bowls in several sizes ranging from small to large (Want to get fancy? Find the ones with spouts for easy, mess-free pouring.)
- loaf pan
- measuring cups
- measuring spoons
- offset spatulas for frosting cakes
- oven thermometer
- pastry brush or cooking brush
- piping bags and assorted tips (a standard eight-piece tip set works great!).
- rubber spatulas
- standard ice cream scooper, with trigger release, for cupcake batter
- toothpicks, for testing cake readiness
- whisk
- wire racks
- wooden spoons
- zester

Final Words of Advice

- Read a recipe from top to bottom before starting.

- Set out all ingredients in their proper measurements and at their proper temperatures before starting.

- Don't swap ingredients without trying the recipe all the way through once. Substitutions can sometimes be a recipe for disaster, pun intended.

- Use the standard scoop-and-level technique when measuring your dry ingredients, like flour and sugar. This technique was used in every recipe in the book.

- Check your leavening to ensure it still activates (see p. 22) before starting.

- Scrape down the sides and bottom of the bowl while mixing, just to make sure everything is incorporated.

- Place your oven racks in the center of the oven to ensure even heat distribution and baking.

- Never overbake your cakes. Check them a few minutes before the time is up just to ensure this. All ovens are different and baking times may vary, so I recommend an oven thermometer.

- When cooling your cakes, lightly cover them with foil or plastic wrap so they do not dry out.

- Don't frost a warm cake. I know it can be quite tempting, but wait until the cake is completely cooled, or you might have a big mess on your hands.

- Don't focus on being perfect; focus on being relaxed and free.

Have fun! Isn't that what it's all about?

CHAPTER 1

POUND
CAKES

pound CAKES

T HE FIRST RECIPE I EVER LEARNED TO bake was a pound cake, and I learned it from my mother. It really has sentimental value, as it was the catalyst for my desire to develop my own recipes. There is something so pure and classic about a pound cake's texture, structure, and taste. The simplicity of it is endearing, but its delightful presentation always fools people into thinking more time was spent creating it. Somehow, a pound cake magically transports you back to an uncomplicated era, when a rusted Bundt pan filled with silky batter, baked at a low temperature, could be transformed into a delicacy worthy of having company over for.

Mama's 7UP Pound Cake

SERVES 12–16

T HIS IS A VINTAGE RECIPE THAT HAS been in my family for decades. It was actually the very first cake I ever learned to bake, which I suspect is not only because it is my mother's absolute favorite cake but also because it was an unintimidating induction into the baking world, with results that even a nine-year-old girl could master. If you are a beginner baker, this is an excellent recipe to start your journey with. You may even get bitten by the baking bug like I did. Mama's 7UP Pound Cake is a classic and decadent treat complemented by the subtle flavor of citrus soda. The juxtaposition of the crunchy crust to the moist inner texture makes this cake simply irresistible. It melts as soon as you taste it.

Grandbaby Notes: *This recipe doesn't have a leavening agent, but it doesn't need one. A significantly longer creaming process adds more air to the batter, giving it the lift it needs. Don't skip this step. The results are a golden-brown, perfectly filled-out cake, no leavening necessary.*

My mother has always been adamant about using the original 7UP and nothing else. She says you can really taste the difference. While I have used other lemon-lime soda brands ranging from Sprite to Sierra Mist, I try my best to follow my mother's advice.

INGREDIENTS

CAKE
- 1½ cups (3 sticks) unsalted butter, room temperature
- 3 cups granulated sugar
- 1 teaspoon salt
- 5 large eggs, room temperature
- 3 cups sifted cake flour
- ½ cup 7UP soda, room temperature
- 1 tablespoon lemon extract

GLAZE
- 1 cup confectioners' sugar
- 3 tablespoons 7UP soda
- ½ teaspoon lemon extract

FOR THE CAKE

Preheat your oven to 315°F. Prepare a 10-cup Bundt pan with the nonstick method of your choice.

In the bowl of your stand mixer fitted with the whisk attachment, beat the butter for 2 minutes on high speed. Slowly add the sugar and salt. Cream together for an additional 7 minutes, until very pale yellow and fluffy. Add the eggs 1 at a time, combining well after each addition and scraping down the sides and bottom of the bowl as needed.

Turn your mixer down to its lowest speed and slowly add the flour in 2 batches. Be careful not to overbeat. Pour in the 7UP and lemon extract. Scrape down the sides and bottom of the bowl and mix the batter until just combined. Be careful not to overmix.

Pour the batter into the prepared pan and bake for 75 to 85 minutes, or until a toothpick inserted into the center of the cake comes out clean.

Let the cake cool in the pan on a wire rack for 10 minutes, then invert onto a serving plate. Let cool to room temperature. Lightly cover the cake with foil or plastic wrap so it does not dry out.

FOR THE GLAZE

In a small bowl, whisk together all the ingredients until the mixture is pourable. When the cake is completely cool, spoon the glaze over the cake and allow it to harden. Serve at room temperature.

Cinnamon Roll Pound Cake

SERVES 12–16

WHEN I WAS 28 YEARS OLD, I MADE MY FIRST BATCH OF HOMEMADE CINNAMON rolls. Better late than never! Before that moment, I loved watching Big Mama make all her yeasty, high-rising rolls without attempting to make them myself. Instead, I ate store-bought honey buns whenever I craved them.

This cake is a tribute to good ol'-fashioned gooey rolls, soft and full like fluffy pillows, piping hot out of the oven, entwined with ribbons of spiced cinnamon sugar, sticky with dripping cream cheese icing—the kind that make you want to slap yo' mama. Don't worry, I don't mean that phrase literally! No one should ever slap his or her mama. I mean that as the ultimate expression of praise and honor of food. If ever one could capture the magic and decadence of cinnamon rolls in a cake, without the intimidating yeast, I think I have. Imagine a moist pound cake with a buttery cinnamon swirl dancing through the batter like a ballerina. Then, top that with the notorious cream cheese icing cinnamon rolls are known for.

Bake this and get ready to slap someone.

INGREDIENTS

CAKE

- 1½ cups (3 sticks) unsalted butter, room temperature
- 2½ cups granulated sugar
- 6 large eggs, room temperature
- 3 cups sifted cake flour
- 1 teaspoon salt
- ½ teaspoon baking soda
- 1 cup sour cream, room temperature
- 2 tablespoons vegetable oil
- 1 tablespoon vanilla extract

CINNAMON SWIRL

- ⅓ cup (5 tablespoons plus 1 teaspoon) unsalted butter, melted
- ⅔ cup packed light brown sugar
- 1 tablespoon all-purpose flour
- 1½ teaspoons ground cinnamon
- 1 teaspoon vanilla extract

ICING

- 2 ounces cream cheese, room temperature
- 2 tablespoons unsalted butter, room temperature
- 1½ cups confectioners' sugar
- ¼ cup milk (can be whole, 2%, or even refrigerated coconut)
- 1 teaspoon vanilla extract

FOR THE CAKE

Preheat your oven to 325°F. Liberally prepare a 12-cup Bundt pan with the nonstick method of your choice.

In the bowl of your stand mixer fitted with the whisk attachment, beat the butter for 1 minute on high speed. Slowly add the granulated sugar. Cream together for an additional 5 minutes, until very pale yellow and fluffy. Add the eggs 1 at a time, combining well after each addition and scraping down the sides and bottom of the bowl as needed.

Turn your mixer down to its lowest speed and slowly add the flour in 2 batches. Add the salt and baking soda. Be careful not to overbeat. Add the sour cream, oil, and vanilla extract. Scrape down the sides and bottom of the bowl and mix the batter until just combined. Be careful not to overmix. Set the batter aside.

FOR THE CINNAMON SWIRL

In a small bowl, whisk together all the ingredients until well combined. Set aside.

TO BAKE

Pour ⅓ of the batter into the prepared pan.

Drizzle ½ of the cinnamon swirl over the batter. Using a butter knife or skewer, swivel the mixture through the cake batter, creating a flourish pattern.

Repeat with the rest of the cake batter and cinnamon swirl. Top with the remaining batter. Bake for 75 to 85 minutes, or until a toothpick inserted into the center of the cake comes out mostly clean.

Let the cake cool in the pan on a wire rack for 10 minutes, then invert onto a serving plate. Let cool to room temperature. Lightly cover the cake with foil or plastic wrap so it does not dry out.

FOR THE ICING

Clean your stand mixer bowl and whisk attachment. Beat the cream cheese and butter for 2 minutes on medium-high speed.

Reduce your mixer speed and carefully add the confectioners' sugar in 2 batches, scraping down the sides and bottom of the bowl as needed. Once the sugar is fully incorporated, turn your mixer back up to medium-high speed. Add the milk and vanilla extract and beat until the icing is smooth and pourable.

Drizzle the icing over the cooled pound cake. Serve at room temperature.

Grandbaby's
Strawberry–Rhubarb Shortcake

SERVES 12–16

....

I ONCE MADE THIS CREAM CHEESE POUND CAKE RECIPE MORE THAN 100 TIMES in a single year. This famous pound cake was lauded all over Chicago (not entirely exaggerating). It all started when I brought one to *EBONY* magazine when I worked there many moons ago. Everyone loved it and started placing orders for birthdays and work anniversaries. Soon word spread across the city (still not exaggerating), and all of a sudden I was making several a week in my tiny Chicago apartment kitchen. My brother André and cousin Roslynn have fondly dubbed it "THE Cake," and it seems to be the only one that matters now. Whenever I have served it—whether it's to men or women, young or old—it always elicits the same response of closed eyes and delightful moans of glee.

The texture of this cake is unlike any other pound cake I have ever tried. It is creamy, dense, and, ironically, light as a feather. You could make this cake and not do another dog-gone thing to it, but I dare you to try it as the base for classic shortcake with fresh whipped cream and strawberry–rhubarb compote, and have your life change forever.

Grandbaby Note: *Rhubarb has a very short seasonal window, in the summer. If it isn't available, try using just strawberries or a mix of raspberries and strawberries. The taste is still fantastic.*

INGREDIENTS

CAKE

- 1½ cups (3 sticks) unsalted butter, room temperature
- 2 tablespoons vegetable shortening
- 1 (8-ounce) package cream cheese, room temperature
- 2¾ cups granulated sugar
- 6 large eggs, room temperature
- 3 cups sifted cake flour
- 1 teaspoon salt
- 1 tablespoon vanilla extract

STRAWBERRY–RHUBARB COMPOTE

- 2 cups fresh strawberries, hulled and sliced
- 1 cup diced fresh rhubarb (cut into ¼-inch pieces)
- ½ cup granulated sugar
- 3 tablespoons water
- Pinch salt
- ¼ teaspoon cornstarch

WHIPPED CREAM

- 2 cups heavy cream, cold
- ⅓ cup confectioners' sugar
- 1 tablespoon vanilla extract

FOR THE CAKE

Preheat your oven to 325°F. Liberally prepare a 10-cup Bundt pan with the nonstick method of your choice.

In the bowl of your stand mixer fitted with the whisk attachment, cream together the butter, shortening, and cream cheese for 2 minutes on high speed. Slowly add the granulated sugar and beat for an additional 6 minutes, until very pale yellow and fluffy. Add the eggs 1 at a time, combining well after each addition and scraping down the sides and bottom of the bowl as needed.

Turn your mixer down to its lowest speed and slowly add the flour in 2 batches. Add the salt. Be careful not to overbeat. Add the vanilla extract. Scrape down the sides and bottom of the bowl and mix the batter until just combined. Be careful not to overmix.

Pour the batter into the prepared pan and bake for 75 to 80 minutes, or until a toothpick inserted into the center of the cake comes out clean.

Cool the pan on a wire rack for 10 minutes, then invert onto a serving plate. Let cool to room temperature. Lightly cover the cake with foil or plastic wrap so it does not dry out.

FOR THE STRAWBERRY-RHUBARB COMPOTE

In a medium saucepan over medium heat, stir together the strawberries, rhubarb, granulated sugar, water, and salt.

Once the mixture starts to boil and the juices begin to release, whisk in the cornstarch. Continue to cook until the compote is thick enough to coat the back of a spoon, about 7 to 11 minutes. Remove from the heat and set aside to cool to room temperature.

FOR THE WHIPPED CREAM

Clean your stand mixer bowl and whisk attachment. Place them in the refrigerator for 15 minutes to get them nice and cold.

Remove the bowl and whisk attachment from the refrigerator. Add the heavy cream and whip on high speed until soft peaks begin to form.

Reduce your mixer speed to medium-low and slowly add the confectioners' sugar and vanilla extract. Once the sugar is fully incorporated, turn your mixer speed back to high and continue to whip until stiff peaks form.

TO ASSEMBLE

Using a serrated knife, gently halve the cake lengthwise so there are top and bottom halves. Remove the top half of the cake and set aside.

Place ⅔ of the whipped cream on the bottom half of the cake. Spread the whipped cream evenly, staying as close to the center of the cake as possible. Top with ⅔ of the compote.

Carefully place the top cake layer over the compote and whipped cream, making sure the filling doesn't ooze everywhere. Finish by spreading the remaining whipped cream and strawberry–rhubarb compote on the top of the cake in a decorative pattern.

Transfer, covered, to the refrigerator. Remove the cake from the refrigerator 30 minutes before serving and let it sit at room temperature until ready to serve.

Cornmeal Pound Cake
with Honey-Butter Glaze

SERVES 12–16

B ACK IN THE DAY, MY BIG DADDY HAD A FARM OVERFLOWING WITH CORN. When it was ready for harvesting, the family would pick it. Big Mama believed in preserving the corn by shucking the cobs, lightly sautéing the kernels, and then freezing the kernels in several bags for convenience. She loved experimenting with adventurous recipes, ranging from fried corn and seasonal corn soups to an innovative corn relish that everyone called "cha cha."

This rustic cornmeal pound cake with its simple honey–butter glaze reminds me of Big Mama's innovative uses of corn in her own kitchen. It is not your average cake; it has a flavor profile all its own, with a faint reminder of the tender and moist cornbread I remember growing up on, which was usually served table side in a cast-iron skillet. For this recipe, I borrowed a page from both the cornbread and pound cake books of my baking past; the two concepts seamlessly blend into something quite special.

Big Mama, Big Daddy, and my uncles Larry (top) and Shawn

INGREDIENTS

CAKE
- ¾ cup (1½ sticks) unsalted butter, room temperature
- 1½ cups granulated sugar
- 3 large eggs, room temperature
- 1 cup sifted all-purpose flour
- ½ cup yellow cornmeal
- ½ teaspoon salt
- ⅓ cup buttermilk, room temperature
- 1 teaspoon vanilla extract

HONEY-BUTTER GLAZE
- 2 tablespoons unsalted butter, melted
- 2 tablespoons honey

FOR THE CAKE

Preheat your oven to 350°F. Liberally prepare a 10-inch cast-iron skillet or round pan with the nonstick method of your choice.

In the bowl of your stand mixer fitted with the whisk attachment, beat the butter for 2 minutes on high speed. Slowly add the sugar. Cream together for an additional 5 minutes, until very pale yellow and fluffy. Add the eggs 1 at a time, combining well after each addition and scraping down the sides and bottom of the bowl as needed.

Turn your mixer down to its lowest speed and slowly add the flour and cornmeal in 2 batches. Add the salt. Be careful not to overbeat. Pour in the buttermilk and vanilla extract. Scrape down the sides and bottom of the bowl and mix the batter until just combined. Be careful not to overmix.

Pour the batter into the prepared skillet or pan and bake for 35 to 45 minutes, or until a toothpick inserted into the center of the cake comes out clean.

Set aside to slightly cool. Lightly cover the cake with foil or plastic wrap so it does not dry out.

FOR THE HONEY-BUTTER GLAZE

Whisk the butter and honey together until well blended. Serve the cake with the glaze spooned over each portion.

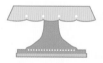

German Chocolate Pound Cake

SERVES 12–16

W HEN I WAS GROWING UP, EVERY CHRISTMAS I WONDERED WHY A GOOD OL'
Southern-raised fella like my daddy had cravings for some random chocolate cake
from Germany. He just absolutely adored it. It wasn't
until my teens that I found out that his beloved
German chocolate cake wasn't German at all (the
name actually comes from chocolate maker Sam
German—go figure!). Over the years, I have watched
my mother make this cake countless times for my
daddy, especially during the holidays. There is just
something so special about the moist chocolate
layers topped with a decadent icing of caramel,
coconut, and pecans. I don't like to mess with per-
fection, but I thought a luscious chocolate Bundt
cake might like to play dress-up with that gorgeous
icing. This cake has all the same elements that
made it popular in the first place, but it's suited up
in a mighty fine new package.

Grandbaby Note: *Don't be leery about the addition
of coffee powder to this cake. It only helps deepen and intensify the chocolate flavor. You won't
taste the coffee at all. I use this trick in all of my chocolate cakes, thanks to Ina Garten, the
Barefoot Contessa.*

INGREDIENTS

CAKE

- ¼ cup semisweet chocolate chips
- 1½ cups (3 sticks) unsalted butter, room temperature
- 2¾ cups granulated sugar
- 5 large eggs, room temperature
- 2¼ cups sifted all-purpose flour
- ¾ cup unsweetened cocoa powder
- ½ teaspoon instant coffee powder
- ½ teaspoon baking powder
- ½ teaspoon salt
- 1⅓ cups buttermilk, room temperature
- 1 tablespoon vanilla extract

ICING

- ¾ cup chopped raw pecans
- ¾ cup evaporated milk
- 4 tablespoons unsalted butter
- ¼ cup packed light brown sugar
- ¼ cup granulated sugar
- 2 large egg yolks
- 1½ cup sweetened coconut flakes
- 1 teaspoon vanilla extract

FOR THE CAKE

Preheat your oven to 325°F. Liberally prepare a 12-cup Bundt pan with the nonstick method of your choice.

Pour the chocolate chips to a medium microwave-safe bowl. Microwave on high for 15 seconds at a time, stirring after each heating interval, until the chocolate is melted.

In the bowl of your stand mixer fitted with the whisk attachment, beat the butter for 2 minutes on high speed. Slowly add the granulated sugar. Cream together for an additional 5 minutes, until very pale yellow and fluffy. Add the eggs 1 at a time, combining well after each addition and scraping down the sides and bottom of the bowl as needed.

Turn your mixer down to its lowest speed and slowly add the flour in 2 batches. Be careful not to overbeat. Add the cocoa powder, coffee powder, baking powder, and salt. Lastly, add the melted chocolate, buttermilk, and vanilla extract. Make sure the chocolate cools slightly so as not to curdle the buttermilk. Scrape down the sides and bottom of the bowl and mix the batter until just combined. Be careful not to overmix.

Pour the batter into the prepared pan and bake for 70 to 80 minutes, or until a toothpick inserted into the center of the cake comes out clean. Check frequently to ensure you do not overbake this cake. Heat oven to 375°F after removing the cake.

Let the cake cool in the pan on a wire rack for 10 minutes, then invert onto a serving plate. Let cool to room temperature. Lightly cover the cake with foil or plastic wrap so it does not dry out.

FOR THE ICING

Line a baking sheet with parchment paper. Add the pecans in 1 layer and bake for 10 to 12 minutes, until lightly toasted.

In a medium saucepan over medium heat, add the evaporated milk, butter, brown sugar, granulated sugar, and egg yolks. Whisk constantly until the mixture has melted together. Continue to cook, whisking occasionally, for about 12 to 15 minutes, or until the mixture bubbles, turns a light amber color, and is thick enough to slightly coat the back of a spoon.

Remove from the heat and stir in the coconut, vanilla extract, and toasted pecans.

Drizzle the icing over the top of the cake. Serve at room temperature.

Kentucky Brown-Butter Cake

SERVES 12–16

Big Mama, Big Daddy, and Great-Aunt Henrietta during a Winona visit

I COME FROM A FAMILY OF BUTTER LOVERS. FROM SOUTHERN-STYLE LUNCHROOM butter cookies and tea cakes to my Great-Aunt Henrietta's famous butter rolls (she was known for these), we are strong believers in the flavor that fresh-churned butter can provide to a dessert. There are few things more impressive than a simple butter cake made with pure, high-quality butter. It gives not only flavor but also richness and tenderness.

This butter cake is the butter cake that has been passed down for generations. I remixed it slightly by browning the butter. You may wonder what kind of a difference browned butter can make, and all I can say is A BIG ONE! The earthy depth, the caramelization, and the golden specks of toasted nuttiness really deepen the deliciousness of this treat. And try your best not to be utterly intoxicated by the fragrance of butter browning in your skillet. I dare you.

INGREDIENTS

CAKE
- 1 cup (2 sticks) unsalted butter
- 2 tablespoons vegetable shortening
- 2 cups granulated sugar
- 4 large eggs, room temperature
- 3 cups sifted cake flour
- 1 teaspoon salt
- 1 teaspoon baking powder
- ½ teaspoon baking soda
- 1 cup buttermilk, room temperature
- 1 tablespoon vanilla extract

BROWN-BUTTER GLAZE
- ⅓ cup (5 tablespoons plus 1 teaspoon) unsalted butter
- ¾ cup granulated sugar
- 3 tablespoons water
- 1 tablespoon vanilla extract

FOR THE CAKE

In a small saucepan over medium heat, melt the butter. Once fully melted, a white foam will begin to appear over the top of the butter. Watch carefully as the butter's color changes from yellow to golden brown and the smell of the butter becomes somewhat nutty. As soon as the butter is an amber-brown color, remove from the heat, pour into another container, bring to room temperature, and cool in the refrigerator until the butter becomes solid again but soft enough to mix. (This can take 1 to 2 hours.)

Once the browned butter is solid, preheat your oven to 325°F. Liberally prepare a 10-cup Bundt pan with the nonstick method of your choice.

In the bowl of your stand mixer fitted with the whisk attachment, beat the browned butter and shortening for 2 minutes on high speed. Slowly add the sugar. Cream together for an additional 5 minutes, until nice and fluffy. Add the eggs 1 at a time, combining well after each addition and scraping down the sides and bottom of the bowl as needed.

Turn your mixer down to its lowest speed and slowly add the flour in 2 batches. Add the salt, baking powder, and baking soda. Be careful not to overbeat. Pour in the buttermilk and vanilla extract. Scrape down the sides and bottom of the bowl and mix the batter until just combined. Be careful not to overmix.

Pour the batter into the prepared pan and bake for 45 to 55 minutes, or until a toothpick inserted into the center of the cake comes out clean.

Let the cake cool in the pan on a wire rack for 10 minutes, then invert onto a serving plate. Let cool slightly. Lightly cover the cake with foil or plastic wrap so it does not dry out.

FOR THE BROWN-BUTTER GLAZE

While cake cools, brown the butter as you did for the cake. When you remove the butter from the heat, instead of placing it in the refrigerator, immediately whisk in the sugar, water, and vanilla extract. Whisk until smooth.

Using a toothpick or skewer, poke holes all over the warm cake. Pour the glaze over the cake, allowing it to seep in. Serve at room temperature.

Grandbaby Note: When browning the butter, don't be afraid of a few darkened specks cropping up. This is perfectly normal and perfectly delicious. You haven't done a thing wrong, chile!

Aunt Irene's Apricot Nectar Cake (Recipe on p. 50)

Aunt Irene's
Apricot Nectar Cake

SERVES 12–16

pictured on previous page

MY FAMILY'S ORIGINAL APRICOT NECTAR CAKE RECIPE CAME FROM MY daddy's Aunt Irene, who also grew up in Mississippi (and still lives there). My daddy loved reminiscing about attending grade school with his Aunt Irene who was just a few years older than he was. What always sticks out about her in his childhood stories are her gentle kindness and generosity (she always gave him extra money here and there), as well as beautiful cakes. She is quite the baker and frequently makes cakes for family reunions and special occasions. My daddy just loves him some Aunt Irene because she always showed such love to him.

Aunt Irene's original cake is made with a cake mix to speed up the process, but this one is a bit different. I created a golden, from-scratch pound cake recipe with hints of apricot nectar throughout. The flavor deepens with a dash of lemon; the cake is about as sweet and lovely as Aunt Irene herself.

INGREDIENTS

CAKE

- 1½ cups (3 sticks) unsalted butter, room temperature
- 2¾ cups granulated sugar
- 5 large eggs, room temperature
- 3 cups sifted cake flour
- 1 teaspoon salt
- ¾ cup apricot nectar, room temperature
- 1 teaspoon lemon extract

GLAZE

- 1 cup confectioners' sugar
- 2 tablespoons apricot nectar, room temperature

FOR THE CAKE

Preheat your oven to 315°F. Liberally prepare a 10-cup Bundt pan with the nonstick method of your choice.

In the bowl of your stand mixer fitted with the whisk attachment, add the butter and beat for 2 minutes on high speed. Slowly add the granulated sugar. Cream together for an additional 5 minutes, until very pale yellow and fluffy. Add the eggs 1 at a time, combining well after each addition and scraping down the sides and bottom of the bowl as needed.

Turn your mixer down to its lowest speed and slowly add the flour in 2 batches then add the salt. Be careful not to overbeat. Add the apricot nectar and lemon extract. Scrape down the sides and bottom of the bowl and mix the batter until just combined. Be careful not to overmix.

Pour the batter into the prepared pan and bake for 75 to 85 minutes, or until a toothpick inserted into the center of the cake comes out clean.

Let the cake cool in the pan on a wire rack for 10 minutes, then invert onto a serving plate. Let cool to room temperature. Lightly cover the cake with foil or plastic wrap so it does not dry out.

FOR THE GLAZE

In a medium bowl, whisk together the confectioners' sugar and apricot nectar until smooth and pourable.

Lightly drizzle over the top of the cake. Serve at room temperature.

Pineapple Upside-Down Hummingbird Pound Cake

SERVES 12–16

THE HUMMINGBIRD CAKE, MADE WITH RIPE BANANAS, PINEAPPLE, AND NUTS, is quite the traditional Southern dessert. The passed-down tale is that the name came from people humming when they tasted the cake. I can believe that, as I have been known to hum whenever I taste my family's version.

By merging the hummingbird cake with another Southern classic, pineapple upside-down cake, and packaging it as a pound cake, I created this dessert to celebrate my family's Southern roots in a unique way. I look forward to one day passing this recipe down and sharing the story of its creation with my children.

Big Mama and her siblings Eddie, Henrietta, and Melzina

Grandbaby Notes: *This cake tastes great warm, before the syrup from the brown sugar and pineapple settles, so feel free to serve before it cools, if you like. A scoop of vanilla ice cream tastes especially nice over a warm slice.*

This recipe calls for toasted pecans. To toast, simply place them in a single layer on a parchment-lined baking sheet. Bake at 425°F for six to nine minutes, or until golden brown.

INGREDIENTS

3 cups sifted cake flour

2⅓ cups granulated sugar

1 teaspoon baking soda

1 teaspoon ground cinnamon

1 teaspoon salt

3 large eggs, room temperature

1½ cups mashed ripe bananas

1 cup canned crushed pineapple, with juice

1 cup vegetable oil

½ cup sour cream, room temperature

1 tablespoon vanilla extract

1 cup chopped pecans, toasted

2 tablespoons unsalted butter, melted

⅓ cup packed light brown sugar

6 whole canned pineapple rings in natural juices (not heavy syrup)

6 maraschino cherries

Preheat your oven to 350°F. Prepare a 10-cup Bundt pan with the nonstick method of your choice.

In the bowl of your stand mixer fitted with the whisk attachment, combine the flour, granulated sugar, baking soda, cinnamon, and salt on low speed until combined. Be careful not to overbeat. Add the eggs 1 at a time, combining well after each addition and scraping down the sides and bottom of the bowl as needed. Add the mashed bananas, crushed pineapple, oil, sour cream, and vanilla extract. Scrape down the sides and bottom of the bowl and mix the batter until just combined. Be careful not to overmix.

Turn off your mixer and carefully fold in the chopped pecans. Set the batter aside.

Pour the melted butter into the prepared pan. Sprinkle in the brown sugar. Line the bottom of the pan with the pineapple rings and add 1 cherry to the center of each ring. Pour in the batter, making sure to evenly and carefully cover the pineapple rings. Bake for 50 to 60 minutes, or until a toothpick inserted into the center of the cake comes out clean.

Let the cake cool in the pan on a wire rack for 10 minutes, then invert onto a serving plate. Serve warm or at room temperature.

Johnnie Mae's
Seven-Flavor Pound Cake

SERVES 12–16

MY COUSIN JOHNNIE MAE, GREAT-AUNT HENRIETTA'S DAUGHTER, COULD BE characterized as feisty and quite fun. Her personality brims with spirit, sincerity, and a "tell it like it is" attitude that will charm the pants off of you. She is all of that and one heck of a cook and baker—just ask her husband, Irvin.

It was only appropriate that, of her many recipes, I share this one. With its unique flavors that meld together in sweet harmony, it's a perfect representation of my cousin's many wonderful qualities and her deep love of life and family. If you are looking for a classic cake with a touch of spunk, you've found it in this dense yet perfectly light cream cheese cake, thanks to Johnnie Mae.

Johnnie Mae and Irvin Wilson

Grandbaby Note: *This cake is certainly not for lightweights. The combination of seven different flavor extracts can pack a mighty intense blow. Feel free to scale back and use a few of the flavors you prefer instead of all of them at once. Or, scale up if you want. Johnnie Mae's original recipe calls for one tablespoon of every extract.*

INGREDIENTS

1 (8-ounce) package cream cheese, room temperature

1½ cups (3 sticks) unsalted butter, room temperature

2 tablespoons shortening

3 cups granulated sugar

1 teaspoon salt

6 large eggs, room temperature

3 cups sifted cake flour

1 tablespoon vanilla extract

1 teaspoon lemon extract

1 teaspoon pineapple extract

1 teaspoon orange extract

1 teaspoon banana extract

½ teaspoon almond extract

½ teaspoon coconut extract

Preheat your oven to 325°F. Liberally prepare a 10-cup Bundt pan with the nonstick method of your choice.

In the bowl of your stand mixer fitted with the whisk attachment, add the cream cheese, butter, and shortening and beat for 2 minutes on high speed. Slowly add the sugar and salt. Cream together for an additional 5 minutes, until very pale yellow and fluffy. Add the eggs 1 at a time, combining well after each addition and scraping down the sides and bottom of the bowl as needed.

Turn your mixer down to its lowest speed and slowly add the flour in 2 batches. Be careful not to overbeat. Add all of the extracts. Scrape down the sides and bottom of the bowl and mix the batter until just combined. Be careful not to overmix.

Pour the batter into the prepared pan and bake for 80 to 90 minutes, or until a toothpick inserted into the center of the cake comes out clean.

Let the cake cool in the pan on a wire rack for 10 minutes, then invert onto a serving plate. Let cool to room temperature. Lightly cover the cake with foil or plastic wrap so it does not dry out. Serve.

LAYER
CAKES

layer CAKES

THE CLASSIC LAYER CAKE IS A SIGHT TO BEHOLD. Tiers of moist cake stacked higher and higher and then cloaked in fluffy buttercream become the most precious monument of any special occasion. The first layer cakes I learned to bake were classics, like rich chocolate and buttery yellow. Both are still the backbones of my collection, but in this chapter, you will find classics remixed with a bit of edge. I realize that layer cakes may seem intimidating, but trust me when I say you don't have to be a type A perfectionist to master them.

I generally subscribe to my Big Mama's school of thought when it comes to presentation. These creations have more of a rustic aesthetic, like the old-fashioned country cakes I grew up eating. I don't believe your cakes need to look like they just stepped out of a high-end bakery for anyone to enjoy them. Simply put, prissy cakes ain't my thang. A cake with a crease here and a dent there in the frosting adds character and is exactly what a homemade cake should look like in the end. So dive right in and remember that while these cakes may require more patience and time, the results are astonishing and well worth the extra effort.

Classic Yellow Cake
with Whipped Chocolate Frosting

SERVES 18–22

TRUST ME, THIS TRADITIONAL YELLOW CAKE IS NO plain Jane—in fact, it's an icon. What makes this cake so special are its classic flavors and staying power.

This recipe has evolved quite a bit from the original one Big Mama developed. I have been tinkering, testing, and perfecting it for years, and I am proud to say that my rendition yields a simple yet delicious canary-yellow cake that's moist, tender, and bursting with the rich taste of fresh butter, eggs, and vanilla. It is the ideal backdrop for a fluffy yet smooth chocolate frosting. While there are tons of recipes for yellow cake with chocolate frosting out there, this one brings home that nostalgic flavor you remember, with the added payoff that only baking from scratch can give.

Grandbaby Notes: *This cake is fantastic as is but absolutely heavenly when you use high-quality butter.*

If you ever want to lighten this cake, you can use Greek yogurt or even milk instead of the sour cream.

If you have some extra time on your hands, separate the eggs and whip the whites into stiff peaks. Add just the egg yolks in place of the whole eggs when making the batter. After the batter is mixed, gently fold in the egg whites. The baking time is a bit longer (30 to 38 minutes), but the result is a very light texture.

INGREDIENTS

CAKE

- 1 cup (2 sticks) unsalted butter, room temperature
- 2½ cups granulated sugar
- 7 large eggs, room temperature
- 3 cups sifted cake flour
- 1 teaspoon salt
- ½ teaspoon baking powder
- ½ teaspoon baking soda
- 1 cup sour cream, room temperature
- ⅓ cup vegetable oil
- 1 tablespoon vanilla extract

FROSTING

- ¾ cup (1½ sticks) unsalted butter, room temperature
- 5 cups confectioners' sugar
- 1 cup unsweetened cocoa powder
- Pinch salt
- 1 cup heavy cream, cold
- 1 tablespoon vanilla extract

FOR THE CAKE

Preheat your oven to 325°F. Liberally prepare 3 9-inch round cake pans with the nonstick method of your choice. (I recommend the parchment method described on p. 17.)

In the bowl of your stand mixer fitted with the whisk attachment, beat the butter for 2 minutes on high speed. Slowly add the granulated sugar. Cream together for an additional 5 minutes, until very pale yellow and fluffy. Add the eggs 1 at a time, combining well after each addition and scraping down the sides and bottom of the bowl as needed.

Turn your mixer down to its lowest speed and slowly add the flour in 2 batches. Add the salt, baking powder, and baking soda. Be careful not to overbeat. Add the sour cream, oil, and vanilla extract. Scrape down the sides and bottom of the bowl and mix the batter until just combined. Be careful not to overmix. The finished batter should be pale yellow and have a silky texture.

Evenly pour the batter into the prepared pans and bake for 27 to 32 minutes, or until a tooth-pick inserted into the center of a layer comes out clean—but just barely. It is crucial that this cake not be overbaked! The layers should have a rich golden color and a spongy texture.

Let the layers cool in the pans for 10 minutes, then invert onto wire racks. Let cool to room temperature. Lightly cover the layers with foil or plastic wrap so they do not dry out.

FOR THE FROSTING

In the bowl of your stand mixer fitted with the whisk attachment, add the butter and beat for 2 minutes on high speed.

Turn your mixer down to low speed and slowly add the confectioners' sugar, cocoa powder, and salt.

Once everything is fully incorporated (the frosting will look crumbly), turn your mixer back up to high speed. Add the heavy cream and vanilla extract. Whip until the frosting is fluffy and smooth.

TO ASSEMBLE

Once the layers are completely cooled, place 1 layer on a serving plate. Spread just the top of the layer with ⅓ of the frosting (please refer to the Basic Frosting Instructions on p. 18). Add the second layer and spread with another ⅓ of the frosting. Add the final layer, bottom-side up, and spread with the remaining frosting. Frost the top and the side of the cake. Serve.

Real-Deal Caramel Cake

SERVES 18–22

THIS WAS ONE OF THE VERY FIRST RECIPES I POSTED ON MY WEBSITE, AND IT is still my most popular cake recipe (150,000 pins on Pinterest and counting). It turns out lots of people were starving for (pun intended) an authentic caramel cake recipe to pass down to their families. I can't tell you how many emails I receive about this cake. One lady told me that she had searched high and low for a recipe that would be similar to her grandmother's caramel cake. She grew up on it and was so sad that she missed the opportunity to learn the original recipe before her grandmother passed away. This recipe, however, exceeded all her expectations and made her feel like her grandmother was back in the kitchen. This story truly warmed my heart.

My daddy on his wedding day with Grand Mom Mom (my paternal grandmother), Aunt Beverly, and Uncle Richard

I have tasted many imitations of caramel cake over the years, and they simply will not do after you try this one. This family heirloom has a moist, flavorful yellow cake that is the perfect sponge for the caramel icing, the true star of the party. It doesn't take the quick brown sugar–butterscotch short-cut. In fact, this recipe doesn't shortcut anything. That's exactly why I named it the Real-Deal Caramel Cake. The caramel icing comes from my Aunt Beverly, my daddy's sister, and she definitely gets down in the kitchen. Try this for yourself and finally enjoy the true classic! The search is officially over.

Grandbaby Notes: The caramel is cooked over a lower heat, which makes it easier to avoid burning. It takes a while to come together, but once it does, you will know it was well worth the wait.

This cake is at the Big Mama level because of the difficulty of the caramel. Frosting this cake can also be tough, so a little advanced maneuvering is in order.

CAKE

1   cup (2 sticks) unsalted butter, room temperature

2½   cups granulated sugar

7   large eggs, room temperature

3   cups sifted cake flour

1   teaspoon salt

½   teaspoon baking powder

½   teaspoon baking soda

1   cup sour cream, room temperature

⅓   cup vegetable oil

1   tablespoon vanilla extract

AUNT BEVERLY'S CARAMEL ICING

¾   cup (1½ sticks) unsalted butter

2   (12-ounce) cans evaporated milk

2   cups granulated sugar

    Pinch salt

1   tablespoon vanilla extract

    Whole milk, to thin out the sauce (optional)

FOR THE CAKE

Preheat your oven to 325°F. Liberally prepare 3 9-inch round cake pans with the nonstick method of your choice. (I recommend the parchment method described on p. 17.)

In the bowl of your stand mixer fitted with the whisk attachment, beat the butter for 2 minutes on high speed. Slowly add the sugar. Cream together for an additional 5 minutes, until very pale yellow and fluffy. Add the eggs 1 at a time, combining well after each addition and scraping down the sides and bottom of the bowl as needed.

Turn your mixer down to its lowest speed and slowly add the flour in 2 batches. Add the salt, baking powder, and baking soda. Be careful not to overbeat. Add the sour cream, oil, and vanilla extract. Scrape down the sides and bottom of the bowl and mix the batter until just combined. Be careful not to overmix. The finished batter should be pale yellow and have a silky texture.

Evenly pour the batter into the prepared pans and bake for 27 to 32 minutes, or until a toothpick inserted into the center of a layer comes out clean. Do not overbake. The layers should have a rich golden color and a spongy texture.

Let the layers cool in the pans for 10 minutes, then invert onto wire racks. Let cool to room temperature, at least 1 hour. Lightly cover the layers with foil or plastic wrap so they do not dry out.

FOR AUNT BEVERLY'S CARAMEL ICING

The entire process is documented in a timeline below. Use the times as approximate benchmarks until you get the hang of it. Once you have made the caramel a few times, it will be so easy you can do it in your sleep. The total timeline comes in around 1 hour and 45 minutes.

Phase 1, 0 minutes to 20–30 minutes: In a medium saucepan over medium-low heat, melt the evaporated milk, sugar, butter, and salt. Continue cooking. The butter will begin to separate and create a yellow, oily film.

Phase 2, 20 minutes to 80–90 minutes: This is a very long phase and is actually the bulk of the process. The ingredients begin to come to a slow boil and form bubbles on the surface. Continue cooking. The bubbles will get bigger and bigger over time and become more numerous. You may even wonder if the caramel will ever come together, but don't worry, it certainly will. Stir occasionally.

Phase 3, 80 minutes to 90–95 minutes: A few white clumps will develop on the surface. This is perfectly normal. Just continue to occasionally stir the ingredients to blend everything back together. Around this time, you should also start to see the mixture become a light golden caramel color. It really is almost magical! The deep color will slowly begin to appear, and the caramel liquid will begin to bubble higher in the pot.

Phase 4, 95 minutes to 105–110 minutes: Reduce the heat to low just to ensure you do not burn the caramel. The bubbling will subside into a gentle simmer as everything thickens.

You want the caramel to be a medium amber-brown, thick enough to coat the back of a spoon. Once this happens, remove from the heat and stir in vanilla extract. Allow the caramel to cool and thicken for 10 minutes before assembling your cake. If it thickens too much, simply stir in a bit of whole milk to thin it out. This caramel is an icing, not a buttercream, so don't expect it to have the thickness of a typical frosting. If you end up turning off the heat a little too early (this is usually what happens out of fear of burning it), let it sit a little longer to thicken before you use it.

TO ASSEMBLE

Once the layers are completely cooled, place 1 layer on a serving plate. Stir the caramel after cooling, just to loosen it a bit. Ice just the top of the layer with ⅓ of the caramel (please refer to the Basic Frosting Instructions on p. 18). The icing will drip here and there, but that's fine. Add the second layer and top with another ⅓ of the icing. If the second layer slides a little, just reposition it until the caramel completely settles. Add the final layer, bottom-side up, and ice with the remaining caramel. Ice the top and the side of the cake. Once the caramel completely sets, after about 20 to 30 minutes, serve at room temperature.

Dreamsicle Punch Bowl Cake

SERVES 18–22

WHENEVER I SEE AN ICE CREAM TRUCK DURING THE SUMMER, I'M OVERWHELMED with nostalgia for the Dreamsicle, Creamsicle, and Orangesicle flavors of my childhood. I smile as I instantly recall ordering Popsicles, jumping Double Dutch, chasing fireflies, and playing hide-and-seek and hand-clap games like "Down Down Baby."

These classic Popsicle flavors are even more vibrant and fun in an old-fashioned punch bowl cake. Southern punch bowl cakes, or trifles as they are now more commonly known, are about as vintage a dessert as you can have. Layers of creamy vanilla pound cake, orange juice, orange sherbet, and homemade whipped cream will capture the spirit of your childhood unlike anything else. This recipe feels like a whimsical walk down memory lane, almost like a dream.

Grandbaby Notes: *This cake should be assembled just before serving. You can bake the cake ahead of time, but don't cut it into pieces until you are ready to assemble—otherwise, the cake will dry out.*

Similarly, don't add the ingredients for assembly into the trifle bowl until you are ready to serve. If the finished cake sits too long, it can get soggy as everything melts together.

This cake is best served right away due to the sherbet in the recipe; however, you can refrigerate until ready to serve. Beware of sogginess if you do not serve right away. You have been warned.

INGREDIENTS

CAKE

- ¾ cup (1½ sticks) unsalted butter, room temperature
- 4 ounces cream cheese, room temperature
- 1 tablespoon shortening
- 1½ cups granulated sugar
- 3 large eggs, room temperature
- 1½ cups sifted all-purpose flour
- 1 teaspoon salt
- 1 tablespoon vanilla extract
- 1 teaspoon orange extract

WHIPPED CREAM

- 2 cups heavy cream, cold
- 2 tablespoons confectioners' sugar
- 1 tablespoon vanilla extract

ASSEMBLY

- ½ cup fresh orange juice, divided
- 2 pints orange sherbet, slightly softened, divided

  Orange slices, for garnish

FOR THE CAKE

Preheat your oven to 325°F. Liberally prepare a 9 × 5-inch loaf pan with the nonstick method of your choice.

In the bowl of your stand mixer fitted with the whisk attachment, beat the butter, cream cheese, and shortening on high speed for 2 minutes. Slowly add the granulated sugar. Cream together for an additional 4 minutes, until very pale yellow and fluffy. Add the eggs 1 at a time, combining well after each addition and scraping down the sides and bottom of the bowl as needed.

Turn your mixer down to its lowest speed and slowly add the flour in 2 batches. Add the salt. Be careful not to overbeat. Add the vanilla and orange extracts. Scrape down the sides and bottom of the bowl and mix the batter until just combined. Be careful not to overmix.

Pour the batter into the prepared pan and bake for 45 to 55 minutes, or until a toothpick inserted into the center of the cake comes out mostly clean.

Let the cake cool in the pan for 10 minutes, then invert onto wire racks. Let cool to room temperature. Lightly cover the cake with foil or plastic wrap so it does not dry out.

FOR THE WHIPPED CREAM

Clean the bowl of your stand mixer and whisk attachment. Place them in the refrigerator for 15 minutes to get them nice and cold.

Remove the bowl and whisk attachment from the refrigerator. Add the heavy cream and whip on high speed until soft peaks form.

Turn your mixer down to medium-low speed and slowly add the confectioners' sugar and vanilla extract. Once the sugar is fully incorporated, turn your mixer speed back to high and continue to whip until stiff peaks form.

TO ASSEMBLE

Cut the cake into bite-size (½-inch) pieces. Place ½ of the cake pieces in a trifle bowl, so that the bottom is fully covered. Drizzle with ¼ cup of the orange juice. Using a spatula, spread 1 pint of the sherbet on top of the cake pieces. Top with ½ of the whipped cream. Repeat the process, using the remaining cake pieces, then a drizzle of the remaining orange juice, followed by the remaining sherbet, and then the rest of the whipped cream. Garnish the top of the cake with the orange slices. Serve.

Red Velvet Cake
with Blackberry–Cream Cheese Whipped Frosting

SERVES 18–22

MY DADDY IS THE BIGGEST FAN OF BLACKBERRIES. I GREW UP LISTENING TO his warm tales of eating them during his childhood (back then Daddy was lovingly nicknamed June Baby, not because he was born in June but because he was a junior named after his father). He adored berry picking in his grandmother's backyard. Those ripe goodies would later star in her incredible pies and cobblers, for which she was well known.

Blackberries are one of a kind, quite sweet (the blacker the berry, the sweeter the juice), and, as it turns out, the perfect mates for a classic red velvet cake. Red velvet is the quintessential Southern cake flavor. The richness of the buttermilk batter, with its slight whisper of chocolate, is perfectly offset by a creamy, smooth cream cheese frosting. You can't beat that amazingness—that is, until you swirl the cloud of cream cheese with a violet streak of blackberry compote. The result is not only delicious but also quite dramatic against the white frosting and brick-colored layers. The beauty of this dessert cannot be ignored. In fact, I suggest you bake this cake when you truly want to impress your guests.

Grandbaby Note: I love the earthiness of blackberry seeds in my compote, but if you aren't a fan or you crave a smoother texture, you can simply press the blackberries through a fine-mesh strainer after mashing them in the compote instructions. The seeds will stay in the strainer for you to discard.

INGREDIENTS

CAKE

- 2½ cups sifted all-purpose flour
- 2 cups granulated sugar
- 2 tablespoons unsweetened cocoa powder
- 1 teaspoon baking soda
- 1 teaspoon salt
- 1⅓ cups vegetable oil
- 1 cup buttermilk, room temperature
- 2 large eggs, room temperature
- ¼ cup strong coffee, hot
- 1 tablespoon vanilla extract
- 1 teaspoon apple cider vinegar
- 1 ounce liquid red food coloring

BLACKBERRY COMPOTE

- 3 cups fresh blackberries
- ½ cup granulated sugar
- 3 tablespoons fresh lime juice
- Pinch salt
- ¼ teaspoon cornstarch

CREAM CHEESE WHIPPED FROSTING

- 2 (8-ounce) packages cream cheese, room temperature
- ¾ cup confectioners' sugar
- 1 cup heavy cream, cold
- 1 teaspoon vanilla extract
- Pinch salt
- 1 cup fresh blackberries, for garnish

FOR THE CAKE

Preheat your oven to 325°F. Liberally prepare 3 9-inch round cake pans with the nonstick method of your choice. (I recommend the parchment method described on p. 17.)

In the bowl of your stand mixer fitted with the whisk attachment, add the flour, granulated sugar, cocoa powder, baking soda, and salt and mix on low speed. Slowly add the oil and buttermilk.

Increase the speed to medium-low and add the eggs 1 at a time, combining well after each addition and scraping down the sides and bottom of the bowl as needed. Slowly add the coffee, vanilla extract, vinegar, and food coloring. Scrape down the sides and bottom of the bowl and mix the batter until just combined. Be careful not to overmix.

Evenly pour the batter into the prepared pans and bake for 20 to 27 minutes, or until a toothpick inserted into the center of a layer comes out clean. Do not overbake.

Let the layers cool in the pans for 10 minutes, then invert onto wire racks. Let cool to room temperature. Lightly cover the cakes with foil or plastic wrap so they do not dry out.

FOR THE BLACKBERRY COMPOTE

In a medium saucepan over medium heat, warm the blackberries, granulated sugar, lime juice, and salt. Once the blackberries begin releasing their juices and the liquid begins to boil, after about 8 to 12 minutes, use a pastry cutter or fork to mash ½ of the berries. Leave the rest whole.

Stir in the cornstarch and continue to cook at a boil, allowing the juices to cook down and thicken. The compote is ready when the liquid coats and completely sticks to the back of a spoon. Remove from the heat. Let cool to room temperature.

FOR THE CREAM CHEESE WHIPPED FROSTING

Clean your stand mixer bowl and whisk attachment. Beat the cream cheese on high speed until it begins to thicken and become fluffy.

Turn your mixer down to low speed and carefully add the confectioners' sugar. Once the sugar is fully incorporated, turn your mixer speed back up and continue whipping. Add the heavy cream, vanilla extract, and salt. Continue to whip until the frosting is smooth, light, and fluffy. Refrigerate the buttercream for 30 minutes to firm it up.

TO ASSEMBLE

Once the layers are completely cooled, place 1 layer on a serving plate. Spread just the top with ⅓ of the frosting (please refer to the Basic Frosting Instructions on p. 18). Add ⅓ of the compote over the frosting. Using a butter knife or skewer, swirl the compote into the frosting. Add the second layer and spread with another ⅓ of the frosting. Add ⅓ of the compote, swirling the compote into the frosting again. Add the final layer, bottom-side up, and top with the remaining frosting. Add the rest of the compote and repeat the swirling process. Do not frost the side of the cake. Garnish with the whole blackberries. Serve at room temperature. Store in the refrigerator.

Grandbaby Note: *The cake layers can be quite tender, so feel free to refrigerate them (20 to 30 minutes should do it) to firm them up and make them easier to work with when frosting.*

Mississippi Mudslide Cake

SERVES 18-22

I F THERE WAS ANYONE WHO TAUGHT ME THE TRUE ART OF INDULGENT BAKING, it was my Auntie Rose, my mom's only sister, or as I like to refer to her, my other mother. I spent a ton of time with my auntie because she and my mom are super tight and close (literally, too; my auntie only lives five minutes away from our house). As a child, I never questioned spoiling myself with a huge hunk of Rose's decadent chocolate cake after a special meal; it was her cake that taught me to treat myself to guilty pleasures and seize moments of unadulterated bliss without a shred of guilt.

This Mississippi Mudslide Cake is the cake you bake when you crave pure satisfaction on a plate. It marries the classic Southern flavors of mud pie with the modern notes of one of my favorite cocktails, the mudslide. Irish cream, coffee liqueur, and chocolate are sure to teach you a very valuable lesson indeed: life is short—eat dessert!

INGREDIENTS

CAKE

2	cups granulated sugar
2	large eggs, room temperature
1	cup hot water
½	cup unsweetened cocoa powder
1	teaspoon instant coffee
1	teaspoon salt
2½	cups sifted all-purpose flour
2	teaspoons baking soda
1	teaspoon baking powder
1	cup vegetable oil
1	cup buttermilk, room temperature
1	tablespoon vanilla extract

KAHLÚA WHIPPED CREAM

2	cups heavy cream, cold
½	cup confectioners' sugar
2	tablespoons Baileys Irish Cream liqueur
2	tablespoons Kahlúa liqueur
1	tablespoon unsweetened cocoa powder
½	teaspoon cornstarch

GANACHE

6	ounces bittersweet chocolate chips
½	cup heavy cream, room temperature

ASSEMBLY

1	cup roughly-chopped cream-filled chocolate sandwich cookies, such as Oreos, divided

FOR THE CAKE

Preheat your oven to 350°F. Liberally prepare 3 9-inch round pans with the nonstick method of your choice. (I recommend the parchment method described on p. 17.)

In the bowl of your stand mixer fitted with the whisk attachment, add the granulated sugar and eggs and beat on high speed for 2 to 3 minutes.

Meanwhile, combine the hot water, cocoa powder, instant coffee, and salt. Add this to your mixer.

Turn your mixer down to its lowest speed and slowly add the flour, baking soda, and baking powder. Add the oil, buttermilk, and vanilla extract. Scrape down the sides and bottom of the bowl and mix until just combined. Be careful not to overmix. The batter will be somewhat thin, but this is normal. Do one final swirl of the batter to make sure the oil does not separate.

Evenly pour the batter into the prepared pans and bake for 22 to 25 minutes, or until a toothpick inserted into the center of a layer comes out clean.

Let the cakes cool in the pans for 10 minutes, then invert onto a wire rack. Let cool to room temperature. Lightly cover the cakes with foil or plastic wrap so they do not dry out.

FOR THE KAHLÚA WHIPPED CREAM

Clean your stand mixer bowl and whisk attachment. Place them in the refrigerator for 15 minutes to get them nice and cold.

Remove the bowl and whisk attachment from the refrigerator. Add the heavy cream and whip on high speed until soft peaks begin to form.

Reduce your mixer speed to medium and slowly add the confectioners' sugar, Irish cream, Kahlúa, cocoa powder, and cornstarch. Once everything is fully incorporated, turn your mixer speed back to high and continue to whip until stiff peaks form. Transfer to the refrigerator until it is time to assemble the cake.

FOR THE GANACHE

In a medium microwave-safe bowl, combine the chocolate chips and heavy cream. Microwave on high for 15 seconds at a time, whisking together after each heating interval. Once the chocolate has melted into a shiny, smooth sauce (this takes about 30 to 45 seconds), transfer to the refrigerator for 15 minutes to cool.

TO ASSEMBLE

Once the layers are completely cooled, place 1 layer on a serving plate. Spread just the top of the layer with ⅓ of the whipped cream (please refer to the Basic Frosting Instructions on p. 18). Drizzle ⅓ of the cooled ganache over the whipped cream. Sprinkle with ⅓ of the ground cookies. Add the second layer and spread with another ⅓ of the whipped cream. Drizzle another ⅓ of the cooled ganache over the whipped cream. Sprinkle with another ⅓ of the ground cookies. Add the final layer, bottom-side up, and spread with the remaining whipped cream. Spread the whipped cream on the top of the cake. Do not frost the side of the cake. Drizzle with the remaining ganache. Sprinkle with the remaining ground cookies. Store in the refrigerator until ready to serve.

Grandbaby Notes: *If you are ever looking for a delicious plain chocolate cake, this one is perfect. Pair it with the Whipped Chocolate Frosting on p. 63 for a great classic flavor. I make it every year for my husband, Frederick, on his birthday, and he loves it.*

The cake layers can be quite tender, so feel free to refrigerate them (20 to 30 minutes should do it) to firm them up and make them easier to work with when frosting.

If you ever want to save time, you can always purchase a premade chocolate sauce, or you can bake and freeze the cake layers ahead of time. Just let the layers sit out until they are just cooler than room temperature (so they are still a bit firm) before you are ready to frost.

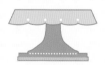

Strawberry Coconut Cake

SERVES 18–22

B IG MAMA'S COCONUT CAKE IS FAMOUS. YOU may think this is a tall tale, but people would literally line up in front of her home just to get one for the holidays. Her cake's highlight is a heavenly meringue frosting, which she whips by hand.

I adore her classic, just like its legions of fans do, but I had a bit of fun updating it. The cake now has an exciting strawberry flavor; the pink layers burst against a bright white frosting with a tangy cream cheese accent. It is such a fantastic way to liven up a coconut cake recipe that has not only been around the block but looks mighty fine for her age, too.

Me and Big Mama

INGREDIENTS

CAKE

2	cups granulated sugar
¾	cup (1½ sticks) unsalted butter, room temperature
2	cups fresh strawberries, hulled
3	large eggs, room temperature
3	cups sifted all-purpose flour
3	teaspoons baking powder
1	teaspoon salt
¾	cup sour cream, room temperature
⅓	cup vegetable oil
1	teaspoon vanilla extract
1	teaspoon strawberry extract
3–4	drops red food coloring (optional)

COCONUT FROSTING

2	(8-ounce) packages cream cheese, room temperature
¾	cup confectioners' sugar
1	cup heavy cream, cold
1	teaspoon vanilla extract
½	teaspoon coconut extract (optional)
	Pinch salt
¾	cup sweetened coconut flakes, for garnish

FOR THE CAKE

Preheat your oven to 350°F. Liberally prepare 3 9-inch round pans with the nonstick method of your choice. (I recommend the parchment method described on p. 17.)

In the bowl of your stand mixer fitted with the whisk attachment, cream together the granulated sugar and butter on medium-high speed until nice and fluffy, about 6 minutes.

Meanwhile, place the strawberries in your food processor and purée until smooth. Set aside.

With your stand mixer running, add the eggs 1 at a time, combining well after each addition and scraping down the sides and bottom of the bowl as needed.

Change your mixer speed to medium-low and add the strawberry purée slowly into the batter. Continue mixing while you tend to the dry ingredients.

In a separate medium bowl, whisk together the flour, baking powder, and salt. Slowly add ½ of the flour mixture to your stand mixer bowl. Continue to mix on low speed to combine.

Meanwhile, in a small bowl, whisk together the sour cream and oil and add to your stand mixer bowl.

Pour in the remaining flour mixture and continue to mix on low until well incorporated. Add the vanilla extract, strawberry extract, and food coloring, if using. Scrape down the sides and bottom of the bowl and mix the batter until just combined. Be careful not to overmix.

Evenly pour the batter into the prepared pans and bake for 23 to 28 minutes, or until a toothpick inserted into the center of a layer comes out clean.

Let the layers cool in the pans for 10 minutes, then invert onto wire racks. Let cool to room temperature. Lightly cover the layers with foil or plastic wrap so they do not dry out.

FOR THE COCONUT FROSTING

Clean your stand mixer bowl and whisk attachment. Beat the cream cheese on high speed until it begins to thicken and become fluffy.

Turn your mixer down to low speed and carefully add the confectioners' sugar. Once the sugar is fully incorporated, turn your mixer speed back to high and continue whipping.

Add the heavy cream; vanilla extract; coconut extract, if using; and salt and continue to mix until a smooth, light, and fluffy frosting is achieved.

TO ASSEMBLE

Once the layers are completely cooled, place 1 layer on a serving plate. Spread just the top of the layer with ⅓ of the frosting (please refer to the Basic Frosting Instructions on p. 18). Add the second layer and spread with another 1/3 of the frosting. Add the final layer, bottom-side up, and spread with the remaining frosting. Frost the top and the side of the cake. Gently pat the side and the top of the cake with coconut flakes. Serve at room temperature.

Peach-Raspberry Cake

SERVES 18-22

THE SIMPLE TASTE AND BEAUTY OF THIS CAKE IS WHAT MAKES IT SO EXQUISITE. It is just lovely, like the ladies in my family. There is something so perfect about the combination of tart raspberries and sweet peaches—here, dreamy pink raspberry mousse stands out against the vanilla cake layers, and a lovely peach buttercream caps the entire thing. It is about as dainty of a cake as you can bake.

To really take this cake over the edge, I add a beautiful ombré effect of light peach melting into a darker mango color. Instructions for creating the ombré buttercream are presented as an option following the recipe.

Big Mama, my mom, Auntie Rose, me, and my cousin Roslynn

INGREDIENTS

RASPBERRY MOUSSE
2 cups fresh raspberries
1½ cups heavy cream, cold
¾ cup confectioners' sugar
1 tablespoon vanilla extract
½ teaspoon cornstarch

CAKE
1 cup (2 sticks) unsalted butter, room temperature
2½ cups granulated sugar
7 large eggs, room temperature
3 cups sifted cake flour
1 teaspoon salt
½ teaspoon baking powder
½ teaspoon baking soda
1 cup sour cream, room temperature
⅓ cup vegetable oil
2 tablespoons vanilla extract

PEACH BUTTERCREAM
1 cup (2 sticks) unsalted butter, room temperature
3 cups confectioners' sugar
¼ cup peach preserves
3 tablespoons cold heavy cream
1 tablespoon vanilla extract
Pinch salt

FOR THE RASPBERRY MOUSSE

Place your stand mixer bowl and whisk attachment in the refrigerator for 15 minutes to get them nice and cold.

In a food processor, purée the raspberries until smooth.

Push the purée through a fine-mesh strainer to remove all the seeds. Measure out ⅓ cup of the strained purée. Set aside.

Remove the bowl and whisk attachment from the refrigerator. Add the heavy cream and whip on high speed until soft peaks form.

Turn your mixer down to medium-low speed and slowly add the confectioners' sugar, vanilla extract, and cornstarch. Once the sugar is fully incorporated, turn your mixer speed back to high and continue to whip until stiff peaks form.

Turn off your mixer. Carefully fold in the raspberry purée with a spatula until well mixed. Transfer the mousse to a medium bowl and refrigerate for at least 1 hour (2 hours is preferred) so it firms up.

FOR THE CAKE

Preheat your oven to 350°F. Liberally prepare 3 9-inch round pans with the nonstick method of your choice. (I recommend the parchment method described on p. 17.)

Clean your stand mixer bowl and whisk attachment. Add the butter and beat for 2 minutes on high speed. Slowly add the granulated sugar. Cream together for an additional 5 minutes, until very pale yellow and fluffy. Add the eggs, 1 at a time, combining well after each addition and scraping down the sides and bottom of the bowl as needed.

Turn your mixer down to its lowest speed and slowly add the flour in 2 batches. Add the salt, baking powder, and baking soda. Be careful not to overbeat. Add the sour cream, oil, and vanilla extract. Mix the batter until just combined. Be careful not to overmix. The finished batter should be pale yellow and have a silky texture.

Evenly pour the batter into the prepared pans and bake for 27 to 32 minutes, or until a toothpick inserted into the center of a layer comes out just barely clean. Be very careful not to overbake! The layers should have a rich golden color and a spongy texture.

Let the layers cool in the pans for 10 minutes, then invert onto wire racks. Let cool to room temperature. Lightly cover the layers with foil or plastic wrap so they do not dry out.

FOR THE PEACH BUTTERCREAM

Clean your stand mixer bowl and whisk attachment. Add the butter and beat on high speed for 2 minutes, until creamy.

Turn your mixer down to low speed and carefully add the confectioners' sugar, peach preserves, heavy cream, vanilla extract, and salt. Increase the speed to medium and continue to beat until smooth and fluffy. If the buttercream isn't stiff enough, feel free to add a bit more confectioners' sugar, or refrigerate it for 30 minutes to firm up before you assemble the cake.

TO ASSEMBLE

Once the layers are completely cooled, place 1 layer on a serving plate. Top with ½ of the chilled raspberry mousse (please refer to the Basic Frosting Instructions on p. 18). Add the second layer and spread with the rest of the raspberry mousse. Add the final layer, bottom-side up. Frost the top and the side of the cake with the buttercream.

Store in the refrigerator until 20 minutes before serving, at which time you can remove the cake to bring it to room temperature. Because the mousse filling has heavy cream in it, leftovers should also be stored in the refrigerator.

OMBRÉ BUTTERCREAM

After you assemble the layers with mousse, before adding the buttercream, refrigerate the cake for about 25 to 30 minutes. The layers should be a bit cold before working with the buttercream. I like to do this so I can avoid doing a crumb coat.

Divide the buttercream evenly among three medium bowls. Set one of the bowls aside (in other words, do not tint it).

Using red and yellow food coloring, create a medium shade of peach in one bowl. Then, using the same red and yellow, create a darker shade of orange in a second bowl by doubling the amount of coloring you used for the medium peach. The orange in the second bowl should be twice as dark as the medium shade of peach.

Using an offset spatula, cover the bottom cake layer with the darkest shade of buttercream. Next, add the middle shade of buttercream to the center cake layer. Lastly, add the untinted buttercream to the top and side of the top cake layer.

Using your spatula, smooth the buttercream around the cake. Clean the spatula with warm water after each pass so the colors don't blend together too much and ruin the effect. There is no need to really blend the colors, as it will naturally happen. That's all folks!

Grandbaby Note: For this cake I use gel food coloring, but liquid food coloring (or any other kind) works fine, too. You can also use whatever colors you like; just make sure you create three very distinct shades so that the difference is noticeable once you frost your cake.

Key Lime Pie Cake

SERVES 18-22

EVERY YEAR, FOR BOTH HIS BIRTHDAY AND FATHER'S DAY, I BAKE MY DADDY A key lime pie–inspired dessert, because key lime pie is his all-time favorite treat. You could say I am quite the daddy's girl—he has always called me his princess, so I guess it was inevitable! Daddy's key lime birthday baking bonanza has become a tradition that he truly looks forward to, and so do I. It gives me a chance to creatively outdo the previous year's dessert.

This cake plays on that creativity by using cake layers baked with graham cracker crumbs in place of the delicious crust we are used to. The flavor of a traditional key lime pie is infused into every aspect of the cake, from the curd filling made with lime juice, egg yolks, and condensed milk to the key lime buttercream, which is perfectly tart when paired with an accent of whipped cream. This is indeed the perfect ode to the dessert my daddy has loved for years.

Grandbaby Note: *To create the graham cracker crumbs, I simply add whole graham crackers to my food processor and grind until fine. Don't feel like doing this step? You can easily find boxed graham cracker crumbs at your local grocery store.*

INGREDIENTS

KEY LIME CURD FILLING

3   large egg yolks
½   cup key lime juice
1   cup sweetened condensed milk
1   teaspoon cornstarch

GRAHAM CRACKER CAKE

1½   cups (3 sticks) unsalted butter, room temperature
¾   cup granulated sugar
¾   cup packed light brown sugar
6   large eggs, room temperature
2½   cups sifted cake flour
1¾   cups fine graham cracker crumbs
1½   teaspoons baking powder
1   teaspoon salt
¾   cup buttermilk
¼   cup plus 1 tablespoon vegetable oil
1   tablespoon vanilla extract

KEY LIME BUTTERCREAM

1   cup (2 sticks) unsalted butter, room temperature
2   (8-ounce) packages cream cheese, room temperature
4   cups confectioners' sugar
3   tablespoons key lime juice
Pinch salt

WHIPPED CREAM

1   cup heavy cream, cold
1   teaspoon confectioners' sugar
½   teaspoon vanilla extract

FOR THE KEY LIME CURD FILLING

In a medium saucepan over medium-low heat, whisk together all of the ingredients. Cook, stirring occasionally, for about 6 to 8 minutes, until the mixture is nice and warm and slightly thickened. The mixture may bubble.

Remove from the heat and transfer to a medium bowl. Cover with a sheet of plastic wrap directly on the curd and refrigerate for at least 2 hours, or until firm and cold. Meanwhile, start the cake.

FOR THE GRAHAM CRACKER CAKE

Preheat your oven to 350°F. Liberally prepare 3 9-inch round pans with the nonstick method of your choice. (I recommend the parchment method described on p. 17.)

In the bowl of your stand mixer fitted with the whisk attachment, beat the butter on high speed for 2 minutes. Slowly add the granulated sugar and brown sugar. Cream together on high speed for an additional 5 minutes, until very pale yellow and fluffy. Add the eggs 1 at a time, combining well after each addition and scraping down the sides and bottom of the bowl as needed.

Turn your mixer down to its lowest speed and slowly add the flour in 2 batches. Add the graham cracker crumbs, baking powder, and salt. Be careful not to overbeat. Pour in the buttermilk, oil, and vanilla extract. Scrape down the sides and bottom of the bowl and mix the batter until just combined. Be careful not to overmix.

Evenly pour the batter into the prepared baking pans and bake for 23 to 28 minutes, or until a toothpick inserted into the center of a layer comes out just barely clean. It is crucial not to overbake this cake!

Let the layers cool in the pans for 10 minutes, then invert onto wire racks. Let cool to room temperature. Lightly cover the layers with foil or plastic wrap so they do not dry out.

FOR THE KEY LIME BUTTERCREAM

Clean your stand mixer bowl and whisk attachment. Add the butter and cream cheese and beat on high speed for 2 minutes.

Turn your mixer down to low speed and slowly add the confectioners' sugar, key lime juice, and salt. Once everything is fully incorporated, turn your mixer speed back to high and whip until the frosting is fluffy and smooth. Transfer to a medium bowl and refrigerate, covered, for 20 to 30 minutes to firm up.

FOR THE WHIPPED CREAM

Clean your stand mixer bowl and whisk attachment. Place them in the refrigerator for 15 minutes to get them nice and cold.

Remove the bowl and whisk attachment from the refrigerator. Add the heavy cream and whip on high speed until soft peaks begin to form.

Turn your mixer down to medium-low speed and slowly add the confectioners' sugar and vanilla extract. Once the sugar is fully incorporated, turn your mixer speed back to high and continue to whip until stiff peaks form.

TO ASSEMBLE

Once the layers are completely cooled, place 1 layer on a serving plate. Spread just the top with ½ of the filling (please refer to the Basic Frosting Instructions on p. 18). Add the second cake layer and spread with the remaining filling. Add the final layer, bottom-side up, and frost the top and the side of the cake with the buttercream. Using a piping bag, garnish the top of the cake with the whipped cream. Make any kind of decorative pattern you wish. Refrigerate the cake until 20 minutes before serving, then remove and let the cake sit at room temperature to warm up a bit.

SHEET
CAKES

sheet CAKES

S HEET CAKES ALWAYS REMIND ME OF THOMAS FAMILY reunions (Big Mama's maiden name is Thomas). Every summer, generations of the family would gather from far and wide, usually in Chicago or some part of Mississippi, for a weekend of fellowship and fun. The fish fries, dancing to the Isley Brothers (and Biggie Smalls and TLC for the young'ns), games, and banquets complete with delicious homemade sheet cakes and fruit punch were some of the best memories I had growing up. Laughter, stepping to old-school soul music, and photos galore were always ample at Thomas family reunions. You never knew what cousin you were going to run into, or meet for the very first time.

The gatherings renewed our foundation of love, connection, and the deeply rooted traditions of our lineage. Sheet cakes are the cakes you serve when you gather people, especially family. They are homey, comforting, healing, satisfying, and perfect for a crowd. The cakes in this chapter are reinterpretations of the dessert flavors I loved growing up and range from incredibly simple—some are even made with cake mix! Oh the blasphemy!—to more intermediate. Whichever recipe you decide to delve into, these are best served with family over a lot of contagious and quite audible laughter.

P.S. If you want to bake any of these completely from scratch, I've got homemade yellow and chocolate cake mix recipes on pp. 96 and 110 that you can use instead of the store-bought variety.

Original Gooey-Gooey Cake

SERVES 20-24

I'T'S FUNNY HOW A CRAZE CAN BEGIN. A FEW YEARS AGO, THE BAKING WORLD was consumed by a gooey butter cake trend. Little did most people know that this cake was invented decades ago—in St. Louis, not the South. In fact, my mom first received this recipe from my Aunt Beverly, a St. Louis resident, over 20 years ago. She would make it whenever we visited her and her family: my Uncle Richard and my cousins LaKeisha and Raquel.

I can definitely see why the craze caught fire. The cake itself is quite a feat! It is about as easy a baking recipe as there is, but the taste is out-of-this-world good! The bottom layer starts with yellow cake mix, but bakes into a buttery blondie texture that serves as the ideal vehicle for the cream cheese custard topping. I guess you could say that Aunt Beverly was a pioneer in the gooey-cake movement. At least, I like to think so.

Aunt Beverly, me, Grand Mom Mom (my paternal grandmother), André, my cousin LaKeisha, and my cousin Raquel

INGREDIENTS

BOTTOM CAKE LAYER

1   (15.25-ounce) box classic yellow cake mix or 1 recipe From-Scratch Yellow Cake Mix (recipe follows)

½   cup (1 stick) unsalted butter, melted

2   large eggs, room temperature

GOOEY TOP LAYER

2   cups confectioners' sugar

1   (8-ounce) package cream cheese, room temperature

2   large eggs, room temperature

½   teaspoon vanilla extract
    Pinch salt

FOR THE BOTTOM CAKE LAYER

Preheat your oven to 350°F. Liberally prepare a 9 × 13-inch baking pan with the nonstick method of your choice. (I recommend the parchment method described on p. 17.)

In a large bowl, whisk together all the ingredients until combined and thick. Evenly pat the batter into the bottom of the prepared pan.

FOR THE GOOEY TOP LAYER

In the bowl of your stand mixer fitted with the whisk attachment, beat the sugar, cream cheese, eggs, vanilla extract, and salt over low speed. Once the sugar is fully incorporated, turn your mixer speed to high. Continue beating until all ingredients are well blended.

Pour the batter into the prepared pan, on top of the bottom layer, and spread it evenly across the pan using a spatula. Bake for 30 to 35 minutes. The center should still be gooey and will look underbaked.

Let cool on a wire rack for 10 to 15 minutes. Serve in the pan at room temperature.

From-Scratch Yellow Cake Mix

1¾ cups sifted all-purpose flour
1 cup granulated sugar
3 tablespoons unsalted butter, cold
3 tablespoons malt powder or powdered milk
1 teaspoon baking powder
½ teaspoon salt

In a food processor, combine all the ingredients and grind until the butter is fully incorporated and fine crumbs form. Use immediately, or transfer to a resealable plastic bag and store in the freezer until ready to use.

Southern Coca-Cola Cake

20–24 SERVINGS

C OCA-COLA IS THE SOUTH'S SODA OF CHOICE. IT WAS INVENTED RIGHT IN Georgia, whose red soil is still home to the company's headquarters today. Everyone recognizes that vintage red-and-white logo printed on curvy glass bottles with twist caps.

The refreshing carbonated taste works perfectly in this cake, which is traditional Southern baking at its very best. It's gooey, fudgy, and downright decadent. While I love a slice of traditional chocolate cake like anyone else, I really adore this version. The texture literally melts in your mouth, and if you serve it with vanilla ice cream, you will think you have arrived at the pearly gates. It tastes just like an old-fashioned black cow from your favorite ice cream parlor. It is THAT good!

When your spoon sinks into my family's Southern Coca-Cola Cake, you may hear it sighing gleeful *oohs* and *aahs*. The last time I made this, I actually thought I did.

Thomas Family Reunion sheet cake summer of 1988

Grandbaby Note: *Open your Coca-Cola a little early to let the fizzy bubbles calm down. It will be easier to measure when flattened some.*

INGREDIENTS

CAKE

1	cup Coca-Cola
½	cup vegetable oil
½	cup (1 stick) unsalted butter
3	tablespoons unsweetened cocoa powder
½	cup mini marshmallows
2	cups granulated sugar
2	cups sifted all-purpose flour
1	teaspoon salt
2	large eggs, room temperature
½	cup buttermilk, room temperature

2	teaspoons vanilla extract
1	teaspoon baking soda

FROSTING

½	cup (1 stick) unsalted butter
¼	cup mini marshmallows
3	tablespoons unsweetened cocoa powder
3	tablespoons whole milk
3	tablespoons Coca-Cola
1	teaspoon vanilla extract
3	cups confectioners' sugar

FOR THE CAKE

Preheat your oven to 350°F. Liberally prepare a 9 × 13-inch baking pan with the nonstick method of your choice. (I recommend the parchment method described on p. 17.)

In a medium saucepan over medium-high heat, whisk together the Coca-Cola, oil, butter, and cocoa powder. Bring the mixture to a low boil and continue to cook for 1 minute. Remove from the heat and whisk in the mini marshmallows, allowing them to completely melt.

In the bowl of your stand mixer fitted with the whisk attachment, combine the granulated sugar, flour, and salt on low speed. Slowly pour in the hot cola mixture, increase your mixer speed to medium, and continue to beat until all ingredients are just incorporated. Add the eggs 1 at a time, combining well after each addition and scraping down the sides and bottom of the bowl as needed. Add the buttermilk, vanilla extract, and baking soda. Mix the batter until just combined. Do not overmix.

Pour the batter into the prepared pan and spread it out evenly using a spatula. Bake for 25 to 35 minutes, or until a toothpick inserted into the center of the cake comes out moist but mostly clean. Begin the frosting 10 minutes before the cake is done baking.

FOR THE FROSTING

In a medium saucepan over medium heat, melt together the butter, mini marshmallows, cocoa powder, milk, Coca-Cola, and vanilla extract. Whisk a couple of times to combine.

Whisk in the confectioners' sugar, 1 cup at a time, and continue whisking until the mixture is completely smooth, with no lumps. Remove from the heat.

TO ASSEMBLE

Once the cake is done baking, immediately pour the hot frosting over the cake and smooth with a spatula. Let cool for at least 15 minutes before serving. Serve warm or at room temperature.

Marble Texas Sheet Cake

SERVES 20-24

THE TRADITIONAL TEXAS SHEET CAKE IS ABOUT "AS OLD AS METHUSELAH," A saying I heard quite a bit growing up from my mom and Big Mama. It basically means something's old as dirt. I also heard "if a bulldog had hip pockets, it wouldn't have to tuck its tail and run." I still have no clue what that means, but I digress—back to Texas sheet cake.

I love when a classic like this never goes out of style and is always on trend whenever you make it. The traditional recipe is made with all chocolate and melts like butter when you taste it. This rendition has the same tender result but swirls in some vanilla flavor, too. The dramatic marbled effect is not only gorgeous but just plain delicious. With this cake you'll never have to choose between vanilla and chocolate, because now you can have it all!

Grandbaby Note: *The icing can be difficult to work with if you let it sit too long. Make sure you swirl it right away after cooking, or you will have to reheat it a little to liquefy it again.*

INGREDIENTS

CAKE
- 1 cup (2 sticks) unsalted butter
- 1 cup water
- ½ cup vegetable oil
- 2 cups sifted all-purpose flour
- 2 cups granulated sugar
- 1 teaspoon salt
- 2 large eggs, room temperature
- ½ cup buttermilk, room temperature
- 1 teaspoon baking soda
- 2 tablespoons unsweetened cocoa powder

ICING
- ½ cup (1 stick) unsalted butter
- ⅓ cup buttermilk, room temperature
- 3½ cups confectioners' sugar
- 2 teaspoons vanilla extract
- 2 tablespoons unsweetened cocoa powder

FOR THE CAKE

Preheat your oven to 375°F. Liberally prepare an 11 × 17-inch baking pan with the nonstick method of your choice. (I recommend the parchment method described on p. 17.)

In a medium saucepan over high heat, bring the butter, water, and oil to a boil. Once the mixture starts to boil, remove from the heat and set aside.

In the bowl of your stand mixer fitted with the whisk attachment, mix together the flour, granulated sugar, and salt on low speed. Carefully add the hot butter mixture, increase the speed to medium, and mix for 5 to 6 minutes. Add the eggs 1 at a time, combining well after each addition and scraping down the sides and bottom of the bowl as needed. Add the buttermilk and baking soda. Mix the batter until just combined. Be careful not to overmix.

Turn off your mixer and transfer ½ of the batter to a medium bowl. To this bowl, add the cocoa powder and whisk until well combined.

Pour ½ of this chocolate batter into the prepared pan. Follow with ½ of the vanilla batter still in your stand mixer bowl. Using a skewer or butter knife, carefully swirl the two batters together, creating a marble pattern. Repeat this step with the remaining 2 halves of batter. (This process doesn't have to be perfect. Have fun with it!)

Bake for 16 to 21 minutes, or until a toothpick inserted into the center of the cake comes out clean. Let cool to room temperature. Lightly cover the cake with foil or plastic wrap so it does not dry out.

FOR THE ICING

While the cake cools, immediately begin the icing.

In a small saucepan over medium-high heat, bring the butter and buttermilk to a boil. Whisk in the confectioners' sugar and vanilla extract. Stir well and remove from the heat.

Transfer ½ of the icing to a small bowl. To this bowl, add the cocoa powder and whisk until well combined.

TO ASSEMBLE

Moving quickly, before the icing thickens, alternate adding spoonfuls of vanilla and chocolate icing onto the cake. Using a skewer or butter knife, create swirls in the icing like you did with the cake batter. Let the cake cool for at least 15 minutes before serving. Serve at room temperature.

'Nana Pudding Tiramisù Cake

SERVES 18–24

M Y BIG DADDY LOVES 'NANA PUDDING. MY MOM SAYS THAT SHE COOKED SO much of it when she was growing up, she thought she would turn into 'nana pudding herself. When Big Daddy came home from work at Mississippi Power and Light every week-day for lunch, he was greeted with a fresh helping (at his request). The creamy, sweet custard layered with ripe banana slices and softened wafer cookies is as delightfully Southern as a dessert can get.

While the traditional pudding is quite delicious, my favorite rendition of this treat is this mix of Southern and Italian delicacies. Blending the two cultures may seem strange, but it makes perfect sense to me. After I visited Italy for the first time a few years ago, I realized how similar they were: Both cultures show love through meals and pass down generational recipes. No wonder pairing 'nana pudding and tiramisù together just works. My version is low maintenance, without the custard-cooking hoopla, but definitely not short on taste, trust that. I added a bit of sweet rum syrup for good measure. I think Big Daddy would enjoy a bowl of this cake just as much as he loves his pudding.

Grandbaby Notes: *A ladyfinger is a traditional Italian sponge cake shaped like a lanky cookie—or a long finger. You can usually find these in the cookie, baking, or Italian aisle of your local grocery store.*

This recipe includes sliced bananas, which tend to brown quickly. That can look odd when you present and serve this dish. If you wish to prevent this, you can submerge your banana slices in an acid, like fresh citrus juice (lemon, orange, or lime works) for a few minutes. It should not affect the flavor of the overall recipe. While this will help the slices stay brighter longer, they will still brown at some point, so it's best to serve this cake within 48 hours of assembling.

BANANA PUDDING FILLING

- 1 cup heavy cream, cold
- 1 tablespoon confectioners' sugar
- 2 (8-ounce) packages cream cheese, room temperature
- 2⅓ cups whole milk, cold
- 1 (14-ounce) can sweetened condensed milk
- 1 (5-ounce) package instant banana pudding mix
- 1 (5-ounce) package instant vanilla pudding mix
- 1 tablespoon vanilla extract
-   Pinch salt

RUM SAUCE

- ½ cup (1 stick) unsalted butter
- ½ cup packed light brown sugar
- ⅓ cup light rum
- ⅓ cup water
- 1 teaspoon vanilla extract
- ½ teaspoon ground cinnamon

ASSEMBLY

- 1 (17.5-ounce) package ladyfingers
- 4 large bananas, cut into ½-inch slices, plus 1 for garnish
- 12 vanilla wafers, crumbled, for garnish

FOR THE BANANA PUDDING FILLING

In the bowl of your stand mixer fitted with the whisk attachment, whip the heavy cream on high speed until soft peaks begin to form. Add the confectioners' sugar and continue to beat until stiff peaks form. Transfer the whipped cream to a separate bowl and place it in the refrigerator.

Clean your stand mixer bowl and whisk attachment. Add the cream cheese and beat on high speed until nice and fluffy, about 3 minutes. Slowly add the whole milk, sweetened condensed milk, banana pudding mix, vanilla pudding mix, vanilla extract, and salt. Beat until well incorporated.

Turn off your mixer. Remove the whipped cream from the refrigerator and carefully fold ½ of it into the pudding with a spatula. Place the filling and the remaining whipped cream back into refrigerator until ready to use.

FOR THE RUM SAUCE

In a medium saucepan, bring all the ingredients to a boil. Remove from the heat and let cool for 20 minutes.

TO ASSEMBLE

In a 9 × 13-inch baking pan, arrange a full layer of ladyfingers. Drizzle ¼ of the warm sauce over the ladyfingers. Arrange the slices from 2 bananas on top of the ladyfingers and drizzle another ¼ of warm sauce over that. Smooth ½ of the filling on top of the bananas.

Repeat with another layer of the remaining ladyfingers and sauce, the slices from 2 bananas, and the remaining filling. Top the cake with the remaining whipped cream. Smooth the cream out over the cake. Garnish with the crumbled vanilla wafers and slices from 1 banana.

Chill the finished cake in the refrigerator for at least 5 hours before serving (overnight is preferable) to allow time for the ladyfingers to soften. Serve cold. Store in the refrigerator.

Big Daddy with his sisters below and family at my grandparents'
50th wedding anniversary

Snickerdoodle Gooey Cake

SERVES 20–24

MY UNCLE BB (BIVIAN) IS QUITE THE CHARACTER. HE TAUGHT ME A LOT about cooking (along with his wife, Auntie Rose) when I was young, and he's also what I would refer to as my "funny uncle": young at heart and permanently stuck in the 1970s. He loves Maze Featuring Frankie Beverly and the Average White Band and regularly says "dig it" at random times during conversation. Whenever we have family get-togethers, he always ensures that laughter and fun are alive and well. I'm sure you all can relate to a funny uncle in your own family. If the mere thought of him makes you chuckle, you have located the funny uncle.

I set out to create a cake in his honor, which at first was fairly difficult. How could I recreate the rich personality of my Uncle BB and put it in a dessert? Well, I couldn't, because he is one of a kind, that's clear. Instead, I stuck to what he loves: snickerdoodles, which makes sense, because they are reliably delicious but not just your ordinary sugar-and-butter cookie. This gooey cake has the same sugary butter flavor and unique spicy kick of cinnamon and rich butterscotch chips. Just like my Uncle BB, this treat is ready for some fun. Can you dig it?

INGREDIENTS

BOTTOM CAKE LAYER

- 1 (15.25-ounce) box classic yellow cake mix or 1 recipe From-Scratch Yellow Cake Mix (p. 96)
- 2 large eggs, room temperature
- ½ cup (1 stick) unsalted butter, melted, at room temperature
- 1 teaspoon ground cinnamon

GOOEY TOP LAYER

- 2 cups confectioners' sugar
- 1 (8-ounce) package cream cheese, room temperature
- 2 large eggs, room temperature
- ½ teaspoon vanilla extract
- ½ teaspoon ground cinnamon
  Pinch salt
- 1 cup butterscotch chips

FOR THE BOTTOM CAKE LAYER

Preheat your oven to 350°F. Liberally prepare a 9 × 13-inch baking pan with the nonstick method of your choice. (I recommend the parchment method described on p. 17.)

In a medium bowl, whisk together the ingredients. Evenly pat the batter into the bottom of the prepared pan.

FOR THE GOOEY TOP LAYER

In the bowl of your stand mixer fitted with the whisk attachment, beat the sugar, cream cheese, eggs, vanilla extract, cinnamon, and salt on low speed. Once the sugar is fully incorporated, turn your mixer speed to high. Continue beating until all the ingredients are well incorporated. Turn off your mixer and carefully fold in the butterscotch chips.

Pour the batter into the prepared pan, on top of the bottom layer, and spread it evenly across the pan using a spatula. Bake for 27 to 33 minutes. The center should still be gooey and will look underbaked.

Let cool for 10 to 15 minutes before serving. Serve in the pan at room temperature.

Cookies and Cream Gooey Cake

SERVES 20-24

GOOEY CAKE WITH A CHOCOLATE TWIST? That might sound too good to be true, but I specialize in making dessert dreams realities, and that's exactly what you get with this cake. The base is chocolate cake mix with chocolate cream cheese filling, just like a traditional gooey cake, but the top is a deliciously light and fluffy whipped cream with sandwich-cookie accents. In a cinch, you can make this and devour it with your friends and family. Just ask my cousin BJ, a cookies and cream fanatic, who went for thirds and fourths of this cake during testing.

INGREDIENTS

BOTTOM CAKE LAYER

1 (15.25-ounce) box dark chocolate cake mix or 1 recipe From-Scratch Chocolate Cake Mix (recipe follows)

½ cup (1 stick) unsalted butter, melted, room temperature

2 large eggs, room temperature

GOOEY CHOCOLATE LAYER

2 cups confectioners' sugar

1 (8-ounce) package cream cheese, room temperature

2 large eggs, room temperature

3 tablespoons unsweetened cocoa powder

¼ teaspoon instant coffee powder

2 tablespoons unsalted butter, melted

2 teaspoons vanilla extract

Pinch salt

COOKIE-WHIPPED CREAM TOPPING

2 cups heavy cream

2 tablespoons confectioners' sugar

10 cream-filled chocolate sandwich cookies, such as Oreos, crumbled, plus 10–12 whole cookies, cut in half, for garnish

FOR THE BOTTOM CAKE LAYER

Preheat your oven to 350°F. Liberally prepare a 9 × 13-inch baking pan with the nonstick method of your choice. (I recommend the parchment method described on p. 17.)

In a large bowl, whisk together the ingredients until well combined. Evenly pat the batter into the bottom of the prepared pan.

FOR THE GOOEY CHOCOLATE LAYER

In the bowl of your stand mixer fitted with the whisk attachment, beat the sugar, cream cheese, eggs, cocoa powder, and instant coffee powder on low speed. Once the sugar has blended into the ingredients, turn your mixer speed to high. Add the melted butter, vanilla extract, and salt and continue to beat until all the ingredients are well blended.

Pour the batter into the prepared pan, on top of the bottom layer, and spread it evenly across the pan using a spatula. Bake for 27 to 33 minutes. The center should still be gooey and will look underbaked.

Let cool to room temperature in the pan. Lightly cover the cake with foil or plastic wrap so it does not dry out.

FOR THE COOKIE-WHIPPED CREAM TOPPING

Clean your stand mixer bowl and whisk attachment. Place them in the refrigerator for 15 minutes to get them nice and cold.

Remove the bowl and whisk attachment from the refrigerator. Add the heavy cream and sugar and whip on high speed until soft peaks begin to form. Add ½ of the cookie crumbs and beat until stiff peaks form.

TO ASSEMBLE

Spread the whipped cream topping on top of the cooled cake. Sprinkle the cake with the remaining cookie crumbs. Cut the cake into slices. Place a half cookie in the center of each slice. Serve at room temperature.

Store the cake in the refrigerator. Before serving, bring the cake back to room temperature by removing from the refrigerator and letting it sit for 20 to 30 minutes.

From-Scratch Chocolate Cake Mix

1 cup granulated sugar	¼ teaspoon baking powder
½ cup sifted all-purpose flour	¼ teaspoon salt
⅓ cup unsweetened cocoa powder	

In a medium bowl, whisk together the ingredients. Transfer to a resealable plastic bag and store at room temperature until ready to use.

Milky Way Cake

SERVES 20-24

ONE THING I ABSOLUTELY LOVE ABOUT THE SOUTH IS THE GIVING NATURE with which recipes are shared. My Big Mama loves sharing recipes with her church, and the Baptist church ladies of Winona have passed her some incredible gems as well. Whenever I visit, I look around her kitchen to see what old recipes she has stashed away. They can be written on anything from an old scrap of paper to a napkin. This is one of the vintage recipes I discovered this way—I found it written on a ratty piece of paper in the scrappy handwriting of a church lady named Hattie.

For this cake, Milky Way bars are melted in butter and mixed into traditional cake batter. The result is a chewy cake with a slight chocolate flavor. I like to serve it warm with a light dusting of confectioners' sugar or with a scoop of ice cream and a drizzle of caramel. Either way, it is a delectable reminder of the Mississippi church ladies who have some great creativity in the kitchen.

INGREDIENTS

8   (1.72-ounce) Milky Way candy bars

1½ cups (3 sticks) unsalted butter, room temperature, divided

2   cups granulated sugar

4   large eggs, room temperature

2½ cups sifted all-purpose flour

1   teaspoon salt

½   teaspoon baking soda

1½ cups buttermilk, room temperature

2   teaspoons vanilla extract

Confectioners' sugar, chocolate frosting, or ice cream (optional), for serving

Preheat your oven to 350°F. Liberally prepare a 9 × 13-inch baking pan with the nonstick method of your choice. (I recommend the parchment method described on p. 17.)

In a medium saucepan over low heat, melt the Milky Way bars and ½ cup of the butter. Stir frequently until everything blends together. The mixture will be thick, gooey, and somewhat oily. Remove from the heat and set aside.

In the bowl of your stand mixer fitted with the whisk attachment, cream the granulated sugar and remaining 1 cup of butter for 5 minutes on high speed. Add the eggs 1 at a time, combining well after each addition and scraping down the sides and bottom of the bowl as needed.

Turn your mixer down to its lowest speed and add the flour, salt, and baking soda. Be careful not to overbeat. Add the Milky Way mixture, buttermilk, and vanilla extract.

Pour the batter into the prepared pan and bake for 50 to 55 minutes, or until a toothpick inserted into the center of the cake comes out moist but mostly clean.

Let cool slightly. Sprinkle the top with confectioners' sugar, frost with chocolate frosting, or serve warm with ice cream in the pan, as desired.

Cousins Lettie Ann, Johnnie Mae, and Eula Jean and family at reunion banquet the night before family church service.

André's
Buttered Rum and Candied Sweet Potato Crumb Cake

SERVES 20–24

....

I AM HARD-PRESSED TO REMEMBER A TIME WHEN MY FAMILY DIDN'T HAVE candied sweet potatoes or yams on our Sunday dinner menu. My mom certainly makes the best ones, and my big brother, Alvin (whom we call by his middle name, André), adores them. On the stovetop, she lets the potatoes simmer away in sugar and spices until the potatoes soften and the sugar and spices thicken into a sweet syrup. I seriously have to make quick moves if I want seconds before André eats them all. You snooze, you lose. Leave it to my big bro to polish them off and then make fun of me for missing another helping.

Adding the rich flavor of André's favorite treat to this cake seemed like a no-brainer. The sweet potato flavor manages to stand out while also being understated, sort of like my brother himself, who is mostly quiet and unassuming but extraordinary underneath it all. The spices further enhance the flavor, and the cinnamon streusel that swirls through the batter and tops the cake adds a lovely crunch. The real kicker is the subtle butter–rum sauce that seeps into the finished cake. I could enjoy this cake with a cup of tea for breakfast or serve it after Sunday dinner. My brother certainly approved once he tasted this winner.

Grandbaby Notes: *If you want to save on ingredients, pick up some pumpkin pie spice and use 1½ to 2 teaspoons in place of the ground cinnamon, nutmeg, and cloves.*

To make sure your egg whites will whip to stiff peaks, be careful when separating your eggs. Egg whites can be quite finicky, so the slightest amount of fat from the yolk can throw off the process.

STREUSEL

¾ cup all-purpose flour

¾ cup granulated sugar

½ cup packed light brown sugar

1 tablespoon ground cinnamon

6 tablespoons unsalted butter, melted

CAKE

4 large eggs, whites and yolks separated, room temperature

2 cups granulated sugar

1 cup vegetable oil

2 large sweet potatoes, roasted, peeled, and mashed

⅓ cup hot water

1 tablespoon vanilla extract

2 cups sifted all-purpose flour

2¼ teaspoons baking powder

½ teaspoon baking soda

1 teaspoon ground cinnamon

1 teaspoon ground cloves

1 teaspoon salt

½ teaspoon ground nutmeg

BUTTER-RUM SAUCE

½ cup granulated sugar

4 tablespoons unsalted butter

2 tablespoons rum

2 tablespoons water

How to roast sweet potatoes: *Preheat your oven to 400°F. Prick the sweet potatoes with a fork, then rub each with 1 teaspoon of vegetable oil. Individually wrap each potato in foil and place them all on a baking sheet. Bake for 35 to 55 minutes, or until they are nice and soft. This time will vary based on the size of your sweet potatoes. When you can easily squeeze the sweet potatoes and the insides are tender, they are done.*

FOR THE STREUSEL

In a medium bowl, whisk together the flour, granulated sugar, brown sugar, and cinnamon. Slowly whisk in the melted butter, letting it coat the dry ingredients until crumbs are formed. The mixture will seem wet, but this is normal. Pinch pieces together to form more crumbs. Set aside.

FOR THE CAKE

Preheat your oven to 350°F. Liberally prepare a 9 × 13-inch baking pan with the nonstick method of your choice. (I recommend the parchment method described on p. 17.)

In the bowl of your stand mixer fitted with the whisk attachment, beat the egg whites on high speed until stiff peaks form. Transfer the whipped egg whites to a small bowl and place in the refrigerator.

Clean your stand mixer bowl and whisk attachment. Beat the granulated sugar and oil on medium-high speed until combined. Add the egg yolks 1 at a time, combining well after each addition and scraping down the sides and bottom of the bowl as needed. Add the sweet potatoes, hot water, and vanilla extract and beat for another 3 to 4 minutes.

Turn your mixer down to its lowest speed and carefully add the flour, baking powder, cinnamon, cloves, salt, baking soda, and nutmeg. Mix the batter until just combined. Be careful not to overmix. Remove the egg whites from the refrigerator and gently fold them into the batter.

Pour ½ of the batter into the prepared pan. Cover with ½ of the streusel. Repeat with the remaining batter and streusel. Bake for 55 to 65 minutes, or until a toothpick inserted into the center of the cake comes out moist but mostly clean.

Let cool in the pan for 10 minutes. Poke the top of the cake in various locations with a toothpick. Lightly cover the cake with foil or plastic wrap so it does not dry out. While the cake continues to cool, prepare the sauce.

FOR THE BUTTER–RUM SAUCE

In a medium saucepan over medium heat, bring the granulated sugar, butter, rum, and water to a boil. Once at a boil, whisk until the sauce thickens, about 3 to 5 minutes. When the sauce can thickly coat the back of a spoon, remove from the heat and let cool for 10 to 15 minutes.

Pour the sauce over the warm cake. Serve at room temperature.

BABY
CAKES

baby CAKES

WHAT ARE BABY CAKES? ANYTHING IN THE mini-cake family, from cupcakes to mini cakes known as cakelettes. The cupcake may be trendy to some, but it's got a rich history with my kin.

Big Mama was quite the entertainer in her day, with a whimsical imagination to boot. She would develop miniature desserts in cutesy packages whenever company was coming over. My Auntie Rose inherited that fanciful gene as well; she loves coming up with fresh new ways to craft and decorate her treats. She is a true visionary. I secretly think she missed her calling as the next Martha Stewart. I know I acquired a lot of my playfulness and inventiveness in the kitchen from both Auntie Rose and Big Mama.

These baby cakes are filled with Southern-inspired flavors and a heaping tablespoon of sweet charm. They are perfect for entertaining, just like Big Mama did back in the day. The only downside is you might end up eating a few too many of these delicious babies.

Pineapple Upside-Down Cupcakes

MAKES 16–20

P INEAPPLE UPSIDE-DOWN CAKE WAS SERVED COUNTLESS TIMES IN MY HOUSE. I was always so mesmerized by its magical creation as a child. I would watch the cake rise in the oven, unaware of the glorious surprise that awaited me underneath. When my mom flipped the cake over to reveal the decorative pineapple topping, I would stare in awe. The cake just seemed so special, so sacred.

Sometimes playing around with precious childhood memories can be dangerous, but I loved taking the risk of transforming this oldie into cupcakes. The base is a moist buttermilk cake mildly flavored with rum and pineapple to give it an extra kick. Topping it with a delicate pineapple and cream cheese frosting makes it even better, but the real surprise is underneath: small bits of pineapple are baked into the batter, ready to be devoured with every bite.

Grandbaby Note: Because of the small amount of butter added to the bottoms of the cupcakes, the liners can get a bit greasy. Before serving, just add a fresh liner over the first one.

INGREDIENTS

CUPCAKES

- ⅓ cup (5 tablespoons plus 1 teaspoon) unsalted butter, room temperature
- 1¼ cups granulated sugar
- 3 large eggs, room temperature
- 1⅓ cups sifted all-purpose flour
- ½ teaspoon salt
- ¼ teaspoon baking powder
- ¼ teaspoon baking soda
- ½ cup buttermilk, room temperature
- 1 teaspoon vegetable oil
- ⅓ cup plus 1 teaspoon canned crushed pineapple, with juice, divided
- 1 teaspoon pineapple juice
- 1 teaspoon vanilla extract
- 1 teaspoon rum extract
- 3 tablespoons melted unsalted butter, divided
- ⅓ cup packed light brown sugar, divided

PINEAPPLE AND CREAM CHEESE BUTTERCREAM

- 2½ cups confectioners' sugar, plus more as needed
- 1 cup (2 sticks) unsalted butter, room temperature
- 6 ounces cream cheese, room temperature
- Pinch salt
- 2 tablespoons heavy cream, cold
- 2 teaspoons canned crushed pineapple, with juice
- Pineapple Flowers, for garnish (instructions follow)

FOR THE CUPCAKES

Preheat your oven to 325°F. Line 2 12-well muffin pans with 16 to 20 cupcake liners.

In the bowl of your stand mixer fitted with the whisk attachment, add the butter and beat for 2 minutes on high speed. Slowly add the granulated sugar. Cream together for an additional 5 minutes, until very pale yellow and fluffy. Add the eggs 1 at a time, combining well after each addition and scraping down the sides and bottom of the bowl as needed.

Turn your mixer down to its lowest speed and slowly add the flour in 2 batches. Add the salt, baking powder, and baking soda. Be careful not to overbeat. Pour in the buttermilk, oil, 1 teaspoon of crushed pineapple, pineapple juice, and vanilla and rum extracts. Scrape down the sides and bottom of the bowl and mix the batter until just combined. Be careful not to overmix. The finished batter should be pale yellow and have a silky texture.

Spoon ½ teaspoon of the melted butter into each cupcake liner. Top with 1 teaspoon of brown sugar. Spoon 1 teaspoon of crushed pineapple over the brown sugar in each cupcake liner and spread it around.

Using an ice cream scooper with a trigger release, scoop the batter into each cupcake liner, over the crushed pineapple, so that each liner is ⅔ full. Be careful not to overfill. Bake for 20 to 24 minutes, or until a toothpick inserted into the center of a cupcake comes out barely clean.

Let the cupcakes to cool in the pans for 10 minutes, then transfer to wire racks. Let cool to room temperature. Lightly cover the cupcakes with foil or plastic wrap so they do not dry out.

FOR THE PINEAPPLE AND CREAM CHEESE BUTTERCREAM

Clean your stand mixer bowl and whisk attachment. Add the confectioners' sugar, butter, cream cheese, and salt and mix on low speed until just combined.

Turn your mixer speed to high for 2 minutes. Add the heavy cream and crushed pineapple and mix until smooth. If the buttercream is too loose, add a bit more confectioners' sugar.

Refrigerate the buttercream for 30 minutes.

Frost each cupcake with the buttercream and top with the Pineapple Flowers. Serve.

PINEAPPLE FLOWERS

Preheat your oven to 220°F.

Remove the skin and core from 1 whole pineapple and discard. Slice the pineapple as thinly as you can, until you can almost see through each slice. You need the slices to be as thin as possible.

Thoroughly pat the slices with paper towels until they are completely dry.

Place 1 slice into each well of 2 12-well muffin pans.

Bake for 35 minutes. Turn over each slice, allowing it to form up the well. Bake for another 35 minutes. Check the slices again. If they aren't completely dry, bake for another 15 minutes, checking frequently, until the slices are totally dry.

Let cool completely. Garnish each cupcake with 1 flower.

Roasted-Raspberry Cupcakes

MAKES 20-24

I LOVE RASPBERRIES. WHEN SUMMER COMES AROUND, I REALLY LOOK FORWARD to picking these delicate morsels of goodness that just brim with earthy seeds and juiciness. Staring at their vibrant ruby exterior only makes me more excited to pop them in my mouth.

Big Mama loves playing with berries, and whenever she delves into raspberry territory, it feels like a holiday. Whether it's raspberry preserves tucked inside a layer cake or a simple garnish of berries daintily placed on her buttercream finishes, the berries' delightful character always shines through. A simple cupcake showcasing their allure was essential for this book.

I decided to roast the berries to enhance their tart yet sweet essence. The result is a beautifully rustic cupcake with the undeniable flavor of one of my favorite summer fruits.

Grandbaby Note: The natural color of these cupcakes is a bit darker and looks almost like spice cake. That is why I recommend adding in a little food coloring to brighten them —but this is completely optional.

INGREDIENTS

ROASTED RASPBERRIES
- 3 cups fresh raspberries, divided
- 1 teaspoon granulated sugar

CUPCAKES
- 1¾ cups granulated sugar
- ¾ cup (1½ sticks) unsalted butter, room temperature
- 3 large eggs, room temperature
- 3 cups sifted all-purpose flour
- 1 teaspoon baking powder
- 1 teaspoon baking soda
- ½ teaspoon salt
- ¾ cup sour cream, room temperature

- ½ cup vegetable oil
- 1 teaspoon vanilla extract
- 1 teaspoon raspberry extract
- 3–4 drops red food coloring (optional)

BUTTERCREAM
- 3½ cups confectioners' sugar
- 1 cup (2 sticks) unsalted butter, room temperature
- ½ teaspoon raspberry extract
- Pinch salt
- Fresh raspberries, for garnish (optional)

FOR THE ROASTED RASPBERRIES

Preheat your oven to 450°F. Line a baking sheet with parchment paper.

On one end of the prepared baking sheet, place 2 cups of raspberries in a single layer—this will be for your cupcake batter. One the other end of the baking sheet, place the remaining 1 cup raspberries—this will be for your buttercream. Make sure the 2 sections are well separated. Sprinkle both sections with the granulated sugar.

Bake for 20 minutes, until the juices are just beginning to release. Remove the raspberries from the oven and set aside to cool.

FOR THE CUPCAKES

Reduce your oven temperature to 350°F. If you have a separate oven thermometer, make sure to check it before baking the cupcakes, to ensure the temperature is correct. Because the berries were just roasted at a very high temperature, you don't want to burn or overbake your cupcakes! Line 2 12-well muffin pans with 20 to 24 cupcake liners.

In the bowl of your stand mixer fitted with the whisk attachment, add the granulated sugar and butter and cream together on medium-high speed for about 6 minutes, until very pale yellow and fluffy.

While the butter mixture is beating, add 2 cups of roasted raspberries to your food processor and purée. Pour this mixture through a fine-mesh strainer to remove the seeds. Repeat with the remaining 1 cup of roasted raspberries, keeping the 2 raspberry purées separate.

Add the eggs 1 at a time to your stand mixer bowl, combining well after each addition and scraping down the sides and bottom of the bowl as needed. Reduce your mixer speed to low and mix in the 2 cups of raspberry purée, a small amount at a time.

In a medium bowl, whisk together the flour, baking powder, baking soda, and salt. Slowly add ½ of this flour mixture to your stand mixer bowl. Mix on the lowest speed until combined.

In a small bowl, whisk together the sour cream and oil. Add to your stand mixer bowl.

Add the remaining flour mixture to your stand mixer bowl and mix on low speed until well incorporated. Be careful not to overbeat. Add the vanilla and raspberry extracts and food coloring, if using. Scrape down the sides and bottom of the bowl and mix the batter until just combined. Be careful not to overmix.

Using your ice cream scooper with a trigger release, scoop the batter into the cupcake liners until each is ¾ full. Be careful not to overfill. Bake for 17 to 21 minutes, or until a toothpick inserted into the center of a cupcake comes out mostly clean but still moist.

Let the cupcakes cool in the pans for 10 minutes, then transfer to a wire rack. Let cool to room temperature. Lightly cover the cupcakes with foil or plastic wrap so they do not dry out.

FOR THE BUTTERCREAM

Clean your stand mixer bowl and whisk attachment. Add the confectioners' sugar and butter and mix on low speed, increasing the speed to medium-high once the sugar is fully incorporated. Continue to mix until light and fluffy.

Add the remaining 1 cup of raspberry purée, raspberry extract, and salt and beat until the mixture is cotton-candy pink and the purée is fully incorporated.

Once the cupcakes have cooled completely, frost them with the buttercream. Serve.

Neapolitan Cakelettes

MAKES 10–12

T HE FIRST FLAVOR I EVER FELL IN LOVE WITH WAS STRAWBERRY. WHEN I WAS young, it had to be in everything: strawberry milkshakes, strawberry ice cream cones, strawberry cake, etc., etc. You name it, it had to be strawberry. Then I discovered chocolate and vanilla, and I started buying a scoop of each, in separate cups, from my local ice cream parlor. Later I finally got the genius idea of adding all three flavors together, not realizing that some other genius had had the idea first. Neapolitan had been there, done that. I was seriously late to the party (I was a picky and peculiar eater as a child), but I'm glad I finally arrived.

Chocolate, vanilla, and strawberry are just as much at home in these cakelettes as they are in ice cream. The result is moist, flavorful, and so beautiful. No frosting is necessary—it would just distract you from these special flavors. Just a simple dusting of confectioners' sugar does the trick.

Grandbaby Notes: This recipe was tested in a six-cavity mini Bundt pan with a five-cup total capacity. However, mini Bundt pans can range anywhere from four to five cups. If your pan's total capacity is less than five cups, just reduce the baking time by a few minutes and check on the cakelettes early to prevent them from overbaking.

To melt the strawberry jam, place it in a microwave-safe bowl and heat on high for 20 to 30 seconds until it is runny and thinned.

INGREDIENTS

- ¾ cup (1½ sticks) unsalted butter, room temperature
- 1¼ cups granulated sugar
- 3 large eggs, room temperature
- 1½ cups sifted cake flour
- ½ teaspoon salt
- ¼ teaspoon baking soda
- ½ cup sour cream, room temperature
- 1 tablespoon vegetable oil

- 1 teaspoon vanilla extract
- 2 tablespoons unsweetened cocoa powder
- 3 tablespoons strawberry jam, melted
- 1 teaspoon strawberry extract
- 2–3 drops red food coloring (optional)
- Confectioners' sugar, for sprinkling

Preheat your oven to 325°F. Liberally prepare 2 mini Bundt pans with 5-cup or 6-cup capacity with the nonstick method of your choice.

In the bowl of your stand mixer fitted with the whisk attachment, beat the butter on high speed for 1 minute. Slowly add the granulated sugar. Cream together for an additional 5 minutes, until very pale yellow and fluffy. Add the eggs 1 at a time, combining well after each addition and scraping down the sides and bottom of the bowl as needed.

Turn your mixer down to its lowest speed and slowly add the flour in 2 batches. Add the salt and baking soda. Be careful not to overbeat. Add the sour cream, oil, and vanilla extract. Scrape down the sides and bottom of the bowl and mix the batter until just combined. Be careful not to overmix.

Evenly separate the batter into 3 medium bowls. Set 1 bowl aside.

Whisk the cocoa powder into the second bowl and set aside.

To the third bowl, add the strawberry jam, strawberry extract, and food coloring, if using. Set aside. The strawberry batter will be thinner than the rest of the batters due to the extra liquid, but this is totally fine.

Place alternating tablespoons of all 3 batters into each cavity of your prepared pans, until each cavity is ⅔ full. Start with the vanilla, adding a tablespoon to each cavity, then add the chocolate, followed by the strawberry. Start again with the batters until each cavity is ⅔ full. Be careful not to overfill. Bake for 24 to 28 minutes, or until a toothpick inserted into the center of a cakelette comes out mostly clean but still moist.

Let the cakelettes cool in the pan for 10 minutes, then invert onto a serving plate. Let cool to room temperature. Lightly cover the cakelettes with foil or plastic wrap so they not dry out. Sprinkle with the confectioners' sugar and serve.

Blueberry Pan-cakelettes
with Maple-Cinnamon Glaze

MAKES 10–12

I LOVE THE MORNING, WHEN THAT FIRST MOMENT OF CONSCIOUSNESS PROVIDES a sense of complete calm and peace. I savor this fleeting moment, which is quickly replaced by the busyness of the day.

Mornings at Big Mama and Big Daddy's always began early. The perfume of roasted coffee, homemade biscuits, bacon, eggs, grits, and rice overwhlemed the house as early as six a.m. That was our standard breakfast down South, and while I loved it, as time went on, I was introduced to pancakes, and they changed my life. I'm glad the South loves a good ol'-fashioned hoecake, hot cake, and johnnycake, because I have had some of the best ones below the Mason-Dixon Line. A stack of humble buttermilk flapjacks, with a scoop of churned butter melting down the sides, drizzled in pure maple syrup, is the dish I would probably select as my last meal.

*Sid and Maggie Small
(Big Daddy and Big Mama)*

Each bite of one of these buttermilk pancakelettes, with its hints of cinnamon, maple, and juicy blueberries, is sure to fill your heart with those sweet notes of breakfast with family.

Grandbaby Note: *Make sure you really prepare your pan well. The berries have a tendency to seep to the bottom and get a bit stuck as they bake.*

INGREDIENTS

PAN-CAKELETTES
¾ cup (1½ sticks) unsalted butter, room temperature
1¼ cups granulated sugar
3 large eggs, room temperature
1½ cups sifted cake flour
½ teaspoon salt
¼ teaspoon baking soda
½ cup buttermilk, room temperature
2 tablespoons maple syrup
1 tablespoon vegetable oil
2 teaspoons vanilla extract
1¼ cups fresh blueberries, tossed in ¼ teaspoon all-purpose flour

MAPLE-CINNAMON GLAZE
1 cup confectioners' sugar
¼ teaspoon ground cinnamon
2 tablespoons maple syrup
1 tablespoon melted butter
1–2 tablespoons whole milk, room temperature

FOR THE PAN-CAKELETTES

Preheat your oven to 350°F. Liberally prepare 2 mini Bundt pans with 5-cup capacity with the nonstick method of your choice. (I recommend my homemade nonstick solution on p. 17.)

In the bowl of your stand mixer fitted with the whisk attachment, beat the butter on high speed for 1 minute. Slowly add the granulated sugar. Cream together for an additional 4 minutes, until very pale yellow and fluffy. Add the eggs 1 at a time, combining well after each addition and scraping down the sides and bottom of the bowl as needed.

Turn your mixer down to its lowest speed and slowly add the flour in 2 batches. Add the salt and baking soda. Be careful not to overbeat. Add the buttermilk, maple syrup, oil, and vanilla extract. Scrape down the sides and bottom of the bowl and mix the batter until just combined. Be careful not to overmix.

Turn off your mixer and gently fold in the blueberries.

Evenly pour the batter into the prepared pans until each cavity is ⅔ full. Be careful not to overfill. Bake for 22 to 27 minutes, or until a toothpick inserted into the center of a pan-cakelette comes out moist but mostly clean.

FOR THE MAPLE-CINNAMON GLAZE

In a medium bowl, whisk together the confectioners' sugar and cinnamon. Add the maple syrup and melted butter and whisk continuously until the mixture is wet, yet thick. Slowly add drops of the milk, whisking after each addition, until the mixture is pourable but still thick. Cover the tops of the cakelettes with the glaze. Serve at room temperature.

Vanilla Bean Crème Brûlée Cupcakes

MAKES 16–20

MY GREAT-AUNTIE MELZINA, WHOM WE CALLED A MENA, WAS THE INSPIRA-tion for this recipe. She was Big Mama's older sister who lived in Chicago. Back in the day when my parents were courting, my daddy moved up to Chicago to attend Northwestern University's dental school after college, leaving my mom in Mississippi. My mom was allowed to visit only if she stayed with A Mena.

A Mena was a beautiful, elegant, and graceful Southern lady tucked in a warm comforting package, just like these cupcakes. She was as fly as they come. The things I remember most about A Mena were her impeccably sharp church suits, polite manners, God-fearing nature, and heavy-handed hugs. She gave a hug like her life depended on it. I never doubted her love.

If ever a cupcake could fill those big shoes, this is the one. The intense vanilla flavor makes these really exceptional. They are a class act with the sophisticated flair of crème brûlée, but underneath the fancy exterior, there is a down-home taste that is as inviting as a hug—a heavy-handed one at that.

Grandbaby Note: *I am in love with vanilla bean paste. It gives you all the flavor of the beans without the scraping. You can use vanilla extract instead, but I highly recommend giving the paste a try for a well-worth-it vanilla explosion without the potential mess of liquids or whole beans.*

INGREDIENTS

PASTRY CUSTARD

- 1½ cups heavy cream
- 5 large egg yolks
- ½ cup granulated sugar
- 1½ teaspoons vanilla bean paste or vanilla extract
- 1 tablespoon all-purpose flour

CUPCAKES

- ½ cup (1 stick) unsalted butter, room temperature
- 1¼ cups granulated sugar
- 3 large eggs, room temperature
- 1½ cups sifted cake flour
- ½ teaspoon salt
- ¼ teaspoon baking powder
- ¼ teaspoon baking soda
- ½ cup sour cream, room temperature
- 1 tablespoon vegetable oil
- 1 tablespoon vanilla bean paste or vanilla extract

ASSEMBLY

- ½ cup granulated sugar
- 1 recipe Curly Garnishes (recipe follows)

FOR THE PASTRY CUSTARD

In a small saucepan over medium heat, whisk together the heavy cream, egg yolks, sugar, and vanilla bean paste. Add the flour and continue to cook until the custard becomes smooth and thick, which can take 15 to 17 minutes. Keep whisking the entire time (it's a nice way to get a workout in before eating these cupcakes).

Remove from the heat and transfer the custard to a medium bowl. Place a sheet of plastic wrap directly onto the custard and refrigerate for at least 2 hours, or until it is cool and has thickened.

FOR THE CUPCAKES

Preheat your oven to 325°F. Line 2 12-well muffin pans with 16 to 20 cupcake liners.

In the bowl of your stand mixer fitted with the whisk attachment, beat the butter for 2 minutes on high speed. Slowly add the sugar. Cream together for an additional 5 minutes, until very pale yellow and fluffy. Add the eggs 1 at a time, combining well after each addition and scraping down the sides and bottom of the bowl as needed.

Turn your mixer down to its lowest speed and slowly add the flour in 2 batches. Add the salt, baking powder, and baking soda. Be careful not to overbeat. Add the sour cream, oil, and vanilla bean paste. Scrape down the sides and bottom of the bowl and mix until just combined. Be careful not to overmix. The finished batter should be pale yellow and have a silky texture.

Using an ice cream scooper with a trigger release, scoop the batter into the cupcake liners until each is ⅔ full. Be careful not to overfill. Bake for 20 to 24 minutes, or until a toothpick inserted into the center of a cupcake comes out barely clean.

Let the cupcakes to cool in the pans for 10 minutes, then transfer to a wire rack. Let cool to room temperature. Lightly cover the cupcakes with foil or plastic wrap so they do not dry out.

TO ASSEMBLE

Place the cooled, firm pastry custard in a piping bag. Pipe a smooth, thick layer of cream on top of each cupcake. (You can also spread the cream onto each cupcake using an offset spatula.)

Sprinkle the tops of the cupcakes with a generous amount of the sugar (about 1 teaspoon for each cupcake), covering the custard. Using a butane torch, heat the tops of the cupcakes until the sugar melts and crystalizes. Garnish each cupcake with a few Curly Garnishes. Serve immediately.

Curly Garnishes

1   cup granulated sugar

½   cup water

½   teaspoon cream of tartar

Line a 9 × 11-inch baking sheet with nonstick aluminum foil.

In a small saucepan over medium-low heat, combine the ingredients. Cook for about 15 to 20 minutes, until the sugar begins to caramelize into a light golden color. As it cooks, use a wet pastry or cooking brush to remove any sugar crystals that form on the side of the saucepan.

Remove from the heat. Using a small metal spoon, ladle out a small amount of the cooked sugar and let it steadily drip onto the prepared baking sheet. The sugar will fall into lines.

Let cool and stiffen for just a few minutes so the curlicues are still pliable, then carefully peel them up and mold them with your fingers. Use to garnish the finished cupcakes.

Rainbow Sherbet Cupcakes

MAKES 16–20

W HEN I WAS GROWING UP, MY FAMILY ATTENDED CHICAGO'S HISTORIC Ebenezer Missionary Baptist Church every Sunday with my Great-Auntie A Mena, which meant we spent almost a full 24-hour period together. I might be exaggerating a tad bit, but it certainly felt that lengthy at times. Church services back then were sooooooooo long and included Sunday school, a four- to five-hour service and long-winded sermon, Mississippi club meetings, and fellowshipping after those meetings with fried chicken and potato salad. This could get quite boring for a child; in fact, I remember nodding off a few times, only to be abruptly awakened by a tap of my mother's hand and a stern look from A Mena.

The times I actually did enjoy church were during the annual summer Teas. The church would erect a huge tent in the parking lot, and I would wear my Sunday best: a frilly pastel-colored dress, ruffle socks or lace tights, and patent-leather shoes. I looked pretty fly, if I do say so myself. At the event, I anticipated one thing more than any other: the frappé, which was ginger ale and psychedelic melted rainbow sherbet in a huge punch bowl. The raspberry, orange, and lime flavors would swirl through the bowl in such a distinctly beautiful pattern. These cupcakes place me right back in that tent.

INGREDIENTS

CUPCAKES

- ⅓ cup (5 tablespoons plus 1 teaspoon) unsalted butter, room temperature
- 1¼ cups granulated sugar
- 3 large eggs, room temperature
- 1⅓ cups sifted all-purpose flour
- 1 teaspoon salt
- ¼ teaspoon baking powder
- ¼ teaspoon baking soda
- 1 cup melted rainbow sherbet (orange, raspberry, and lime flavored)
- 1 teaspoon vegetable oil
- 1 teaspoon orange gelatin powder
- 3 drops red food coloring, divided

- 2 drops yellow food coloring
- 1 teaspoon raspberry gelatin powder
- 1 teaspoon lime gelatin powder
- 3 drops green food coloring

FROSTING

- ½ cup (1 stick) unsalted butter, room temperature
- 1½ cups confectioners' sugar
- 1 tablespoon heavy cream
- 1 teaspoon vanilla extract
- Pinch salt
- Frozen rainbow sherbet, for garnish

FOR THE CUPCAKES

Preheat your oven to 350°F. Line 2 8- or 10-well muffin pans with 16 to 20 cupcake liners.

In the bowl of your stand mixer fitted with the whisk attachment, beat the butter for 2 minutes on high speed. Slowly add the granulated sugar. Cream together for an additional 5 minutes, until very pale yellow and fluffy. Add the eggs 1 at a time, combining well after each addition and scraping down the sides and bottom of the bowl as needed.

Turn your mixer down to its lowest speed and slowly add the flour in 2 batches. Add the salt, baking powder, and baking soda. Be careful not to overbeat. Add the melted sherbet and oil. Scrape down the sides and bottom of the bowl and mix until just combined. The finished batter should be a peachy pale-orange color with a thick texture.

Evenly separate the batter into 3 medium bowls.

To the first bowl, add the orange gelatin, 1 drop of the red food coloring, and the yellow food coloring. Whisk until well combined.

To the second bowl, add the raspberry gelatin and 2 drops of the red food coloring. Whisk until well combined.

To the third bowl, add the lime gelatin and green food coloring. Whisk together until well combined.

Start with the orange, adding a tablespoon to each cupcake liner, then add the raspberry, followed by the lime. Start again with the batters until each cupcake liner is ⅔ full. Be careful not to overfill. Bake for 20 to 24 minutes, or until a toothpick inserted into the center of a cupcake comes out moist but mostly clean.

Let the cupcakes cool in the pans for 10 minutes, then transfer to a wire rack. Let cool to room temperature. Lightly cover the cupcakes with foil or plastic wrap so they do not dry out.

FOR THE FROSTING

Clean your stand mixer bowl and whisk attachment. Add the butter and beat on high speed until light and airy.

Turn your mixer down to low speed and carefully add the confectioners' sugar. Once the sugar is fully incorporated, increase the speed to medium-high. Add the heavy cream, vanilla extract, and salt and continue to mix until fully blended.

TO ASSEMBLE

Using a piping bag, squeeze a wide circle of frosting on each cupcake, leaving space in the center for sherbet.

Using a melon baller, scoop a small ball of frozen sherbet into the center of the frosting. Serve immediately, before the sherbet melts.

Zucchini Cupcakes
with Lemon–Cinnamon Buttercream

MAKES 20-24

COLLARD GREENS, STRING BEANS, CABBAGE, AND SPINACH WERE SOME OF THE green vegetables that would inevitably end up on my Sunday dinner plate next to the smothered chicken and macaroni and cheese. No matter what was on the menu, if it was green, I wasn't a fan at all. When I was old enough to make my own plate, I always skipped the green vegetables (sad but true). It wasn't until I was introduced to zucchini that I actually started to open my mind to anything green. I know zucchini is in the squash family (technically a fruit), but it was as close to kale as I was going to get at that time.

I first had zucchini in buttery sweet bread that tasted more like cake. It was fantastic! I finally realized that if you could mix some greens with butter and sugar, you could definitely get me to eat them. These zucchini cupcakes are just delicious, and the perfect way to get some greens in your system, Grandbaby style.

Grandbaby Note: For a milder flavor, go with vegetable oil. If you want a stronger flavor to complement the zucchini, however, try olive oil. Extra virgin is even stronger. It gives a lovely earthy touch.

INGREDIENTS

CUPCAKES

- 3 cups sifted all-purpose flour
- 1 teaspoon ground cinnamon
- 1 teaspoon salt
- 1 teaspoon baking powder
- ½ teaspoon baking soda
- 2 cups granulated sugar
- 1 cup vegetable or olive oil
- 3 large eggs, room temperature
- 1 cup grated zucchini
- 1 tablespoon vanilla extract
- 1 teaspoon lemon zest

LEMON-CINNAMON BUTTERCREAM

- 1 cup (2 sticks) unsalted butter, room temperature
- 6 ounces cream cheese, room temperature
- 1½ cups confectioners' sugar
- 2 tablespoons heavy cream, cold
- 2 teaspoons lemon extract
- ½ teaspoon lemon zest
- ½ teaspoon ground cinnamon
- Pinch salt

FOR THE CUPCAKES

Preheat your oven to 325°F. Line 2 12-well muffin pans with 20 to 24 cupcake liners.

In the bowl of your stand mixer fitted with the whisk attachment, mix the flour, cinnamon, salt, baking powder, and baking soda on low speed until everything is incorporated.

Increase your mixer speed to medium. Add the granulated sugar, oil, and eggs and mix. Add the grated zucchini, vanilla extract, and lemon zest. Be careful not to overmix.

Using an ice cream scooper with a trigger release, scoop the batter into the cupcake liners until each is ⅔ full. Be careful not to overfill. Bake for 25 to 30 minutes, or until a toothpick inserted into the center of a cupcake comes out mostly clean but still moist.

Let the cupcakes cool in the pans for 10 minutes, then transfer to a wire rack. Let cool to room temperature. Lightly cover the cupcakes with foil or plastic wrap so they do not dry out.

FOR THE BUTTERCREAM

Clean your stand mixer bowl and whisk attachment. Add the butter, cream cheese, and confectioners' sugar and mix on low speed until just combined. Turn your mixer speed to high and beat for 2 minutes. Add the heavy cream, lemon extract, lemon zest, cinnamon, and salt and mix until the buttercream is fluffy.

Once the cupcakes have cooled completely, frost them with the buttercream. Serve.

CHAPTER 5

CELEBRATION
CAKES

celebration CAKES

FROM BIRTHDAYS TO ANNIVERSARIES, OUR life celebrations are what truly matter. Like chapters in a beloved memoir, we revisit these memories time and time again. The pages are tattered and worn, but the moments are as vivid as the day they occurred. In my family, our memoir is breathed in every time we get together. Over dessert, the stories are retold, emotions and laughter swell in the room, and we are transported back to those celebrations.

Each cake in this chapter represents a snapshot of one of those special moments. Big or small, they stand out in my personal memoir and helped shape who I am. Whether you put candles on one of these delights or share one under romantic candlelight, I know that the love injected into these cakes will bring a smile to your face.

And because my Uncle Sonny truly knew how to celebrate this thing we call life, I dedicate this chapter to him.

S'more Lava Cakes

MAKES 4

T HE FIRST TIME I HAD A S'MORE, I WAS AT A GIRL SCOUT CAMP SITTING around the big open fire loudly singing camp songs with my fellow Brownies. Huddled in a circle, we loaded our twigs with fluffy marshmallows to toast them over the crackling fire. Then we stacked them with chocolate and crunchy graham crackers.

Bringing the childhood nostalgia of s'mores to a "mature" lava cake was one of the most genius ideas I have ever had, if I do say so myself. It's quite a pleasant surprise to bite into what seems like a very simple and classic molten cake, only to be greeted with toasted marshmallow and graham cracker decadence oozing out of the center. Now I can always relive that childhood moment right in my own kitchen.

Me during my Girl Scout Daisy years

Grandbaby Notes: *These are best eaten the day they are made and, might I add, right out of the oven while they are still warm and gooey.*

If you don't have a butane torch, you can always stick the finished lava cakes under the broiler for just a few seconds.

INGREDIENTS

1	cup (2 sticks) unsalted butter, divided
½	cup graham cracker crumbs
1½	teaspoons granulated sugar
16	large marshmallows, divided
3	ounces bittersweet chocolate, roughly chopped
¾	cup confectioners' sugar
¼	cup sifted all-purpose flour
½	teaspoon salt
2	large eggs
1	large egg yolk
1½	teaspoons vanilla extract

Prepare 4 6-ounce ramekins with the nonstick method of your choice.

In a small sauté pan over medium heat, melt 2 tablespoons of the butter. Add the graham cracker crumbs and granulated sugar and cook for 2 to 3 minutes, until toasted and golden brown. Remove from the heat and set aside.

Preheat your broiler for 5 minutes. Line a baking sheet with parchment paper.

Place the marshmallows on the prepared baking sheet and broil them until toasted brown but not burned. Watch carefully that the marshmallows hold their shape because this process happens quickly. Remove the marshmallows from the oven and set aside.

Turn off the broiler and preheat your oven to 425°F.

In a medium microwave-safe bowl, place the chocolate and remaining 6 tablespoons of the butter. Heat on high in the microwave in 20-second intervals, stirring after each heating, until the mixture is completely melted and smooth. Whisk in the confectioners' sugar, flour, and salt. Continue to whisk until the batter is thick. It should become more difficult to whisk.

Whisk in the eggs, egg yolk, and vanilla extract and stir well to blend.

Pour the batter into the prepared ramekins until each is ½ full. Place 2 toasted marshmallows into the center of each ramekin.

Evenly distribute ⅓ cup of the toasted graham cracker crumbs over the marshmallows. Spoon in the remaining batter so each ramekin is ¾ full. The marshmallows and graham cracker crumbs should be completely covered with the batter. Bake for 12 to 14 minutes.

Let cool for 2 minutes, then run a butter knife along the inside of each ramekin to help release the cake. Invert the cakes onto individual plates.

Top each cake with 2 of the remaining 8 marshmallows and sprinkle with the remaining graham cracker crumbs. Using a butane torch, brown the tops of the marshmallows. Serve warm.

Earning a new badge as a Brownie

Peach Cobbler Shortcake

SERVES 18–22

P EACH COBBLER IS MY ALL-TIME FAVORITE dessert, hands down, and Big Mama's is a masterpiece. She loved to surprise me with one whenever I visited, and I sometimes surprised myself with how much I could eat in one sitting.

The moment I first tasted peach cobbler was a revelation. Just imagine ripe peaches and syrupy sweetness bubbling beneath the delicate lattice of a buttery and flaky pastry crust. It simply can't get any better.

This cake is all about reinventing my favorite Southern classic with a modern edge. Layers of soft butter cake drenched in spiced peaches and syrup, crunchy brown sugar crumble, decadent caramel sauce, and fluffy whipped cream give peach cobbler a whole new look. This cake is worthy of any celebration.

INGREDIENTS

CAKE

- 1½ cups (3 sticks) unsalted butter, room temperature
- 2½ cups granulated sugar
- 6 large eggs, room temperature
- 3 cups sifted cake flour
- 1 teaspoon salt
- ½ teaspoon baking soda
- 1 cup sour cream, room temperature
- 2 tablespoons vegetable oil
- 1 tablespoon vanilla extract

SAUTÉED PEACHES

- ½ cup (1 stick) unsalted butter
- 4 cups fresh, peeled peach slices
- ½ cup granulated sugar (if the peaches aren't very sweet, go up to ¾ cup)
- ½ teaspoon ground cinnamon
- ¼ teaspoon ground nutmeg
- Pinch salt
- 1 tablespoon vanilla extract

CRUMBLE

- ⅓ cup all-purpose flour
- 3 tablespoons packed light brown sugar
- ½ teaspoon granulated sugar
- ½ teaspoon salt
- ¼ teaspoon ground cinnamon
- 2 tablespoons unsalted butter, melted

CARAMEL SAUCE

- ¾ cup evaporated milk
- ½ cup granulated sugar
- 4 tablespoons unsalted butter
- 1 teaspoon vanilla extract

WHIPPED CREAM

- 4 cups heavy cream, cold
- ⅓ cup confectioners' sugar

FOR THE CAKE

Preheat your oven to 325°F. Liberally prepare 3 9-inch round cake pans with the nonstick method of your choice. (I recommend the parchment method described on p. 17.)

In the bowl of your stand mixer fitted with the whisk attachment, beat the butter on high speed for 1 minute. Slowly add the granulated sugar. Cream together for an additional 5 minutes, until very pale yellow and fluffy. Add the eggs 1 at a time, combining well after each addition and scraping down the sides and bottom of the bowl as needed.

Turn your mixer down to its lowest speed and slowly add the flour in 2 batches. Add the salt and baking soda. Be careful not to overbeat. Add the sour cream, oil, and vanilla extract. Scrape down the sides and bottom of the bowl and mix the batter until just combined. Be careful not to overmix.

Evenly pour the batter into the prepared pans. Bake for 30 to 35 minutes, or until a toothpick inserted into the center of a layer comes out just barely clean. Do not overbake.

The layers will be pale yellow, almost cream colored, and will be rounded and puffed. The puffing will settle and flatten, and the color will become more golden as the layers rest.

Let the layers cool in the pans for 10 minutes, then invert onto wire racks. Let cool for 1 hour. Wrap each layer in plastic wrap and transfer to the freezer to chill for 30 minutes to make them easier to work with when assembling the shortcake.

FOR THE SAUTÉED PEACHES

In a large sauté pan over medium heat, melt the butter. Add the peaches, granulated sugar, cinnamon, nutmeg, and salt and sauté until the peaches are soft and the syrup has reduced by half and thickened, about 15 to 20 minutes.

Remove from the heat, stir in the vanilla extract, and set aside to continue cooling and thickening.

Grandbaby Notes: To peel the peaches, drop them into a large pot of boiling water for about 20 seconds, then quickly move them to an ice-water bath to keep them from cooking through. At that point, the skin should easily peel off.

Peaches not in season? You can substitute frozen peach slices.

FOR THE CRUMBLE

When the layers are done baking, increase the oven temperature to 375°F. Line a baking sheet with parchment paper.

In a medium bowl, whisk together the flour, brown sugar, granulated sugar, salt, and cinnamon until well combined. Slowly add the melted butter and stir to combine, until small crumbs develop.

Spread the crumbs over the prepared baking sheet and bake for 10 to 12 minutes, until crisp and golden. Stir the crumbs after 6 or 7 minutes, just to make sure they don't stick.

Remove the crumbs from the oven and let cool to room temperature.

FOR THE CARAMEL SAUCE

In a small saucepan over medium heat, bring all of the ingredients to a boil, whisking occasionally.

Allow the sauce to boil for 15 to 25 minutes, or until it thickens and turns a light amber color. Once the sauce coats the back of a spoon, remove from the heat. Let cool to room temperature.

FOR THE WHIPPED CREAM

Clean your stand mixer bowl and whisk attachment. Place them in the refrigerator for 15 minutes to get them nice and cold.

Remove the bowl and whisk attachment from the refrigerator. Add the heavy cream and whip on high speed until soft peaks begin to form.

Turn your mixer down to medium-low speed and slowly add the confectioners' sugar. Once the sugar is fully incorporated, turn your mixer speed back to high and continue to whip until stiff peaks form. Set aside.

TO ASSEMBLE

Place a layer on your serving plate. Top with ⅓ of the sautéed peaches. Top the peaches with ⅓ of the whipped cream. Garnish the layer with ⅓ of the crumble and a drizzling of ⅓ of the caramel sauce.

Top the first layer with the second layer and repeat with ⅓ of the peaches, whipped cream, crumble, and caramel sauce.

Top the second cake layer with the third layer, bottom-side up. Top with the remaining peaches, whipped cream, crumble, and caramel sauce. Do not add whipped cream to the side of the cake.

Grandbaby Notes: Don't be intimidated by the many components. With a little planning, the timing works out well. While the layers are baking, you can prepare the peaches. When the layers are done, you can leave the oven on to make the crumble.

You can make the cake layers, peaches, caramel sauce, and whipped cream ahead of time. You can also use a high-quality store-bought caramel sauce if you completely run out of time.

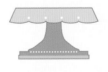

Strawberry Sundae Cake

SERVES 18–22

M Y LOVE OF STRAWBERRY ICE CREAM IS WELL DOCUMENTED AT THIS POINT (see Neapolitan Cakelettes on p. 131). Nothing could keep me from being a hard-core frozen-strawberry groupie. Because I wasn't too adventurous with my eating, once I loved something, I latched on and never let go. Can you blame me, though? I could not get enough of the pretty, pink, luscious sweet cream with bits of fresh berries sprinkled throughout. The fixation began when my daddy started taking our family to an epic ice cream parlor called The Plush Horse after my summer golf lessons at a premier golf course. While my daddy was trying to groom the next Tiger Woods, he instead groomed a frozen-strawberry groupie. I was so hooked that every single ice cream parlor visit until the age of 14 resulted in my walking away with strawberry ice cream.

Auntie Rose, Pat (A Mena's granddaughter), me, my mom, and André

This cake reminds me of those countless visits. Silky fresh-churned strawberry ice cream is sandwiched between moist vanilla cake layers, then the entire thing is frosted with a dreamy whipped cream. Because it's ice cream, it can melt quickly—but that's fine, because this cake won't stick around for long once it's done.

INGREDIENTS

ICE CREAM
- 3 large eggs
- 2 large egg yolks
- 1½ cups granulated sugar
- Pinch salt
- 2 cups heavy cream
- 2 cups half-and-half
- 1 pound fresh strawberries, hulled, puréed with 2 tablespoons granulated sugar
- 2 tablespoons vanilla extract
- 4 drops red food coloring (optional)

CAKE
- 2½ cups granulated sugar
- 1½ cups vegetable oil
- 6 large eggs, room temperature
- 1 large egg white, room temperature
- 2½ cups sifted cake flour
- ⅔ cup malt powder
- 1 teaspoon salt
- ½ teaspoon baking powder
- ½ teaspoon baking soda
- 1 cup buttermilk, room temperature
- 2 tablespoons vanilla extract

WHIPPED CREAM
- 3 cups heavy cream, cold
- 3 tablespoons confectioners' sugar
- 1 teaspoon vanilla extract

FOR THE ICE CREAM

In a medium bowl, whisk together the eggs and egg yolks. Add the granulated sugar and salt and whisk to incorporate.

In a large saucepan over medium heat, bring the heavy cream and half-and-half to a boil. Once the mixture starts to boil, remove from the heat.

Slowly whisk 3 tablespoons of the hot heavy cream mixture into the egg mixture. Whisk constantly to make sure the eggs don't scramble and slowly add the rest of the heavy cream mixture. Add the strawberry purée, vanilla extract, and food coloring, if using, and stir to combine. Refrigerate for 2 to 3 hours.

Remove from the refrigerator. Make ice cream according to your ice cream maker instructions.

While the ice cream churns, line 2 9-inch round cake pans with plastic wrap.

Once the ice cream is at the soft-serve stage, spoon it evenly into the prepared pans and cover the tops with more plastic wrap. Freeze for at least 5 hours, preferably overnight.

FOR THE CAKE

Preheat your oven to 325°F. Liberally prepare 3 9-inch round cake pans with the nonstick method of your choice. (I recommend the parchment method described on p. 17.)

In the bowl of your stand mixer fitted with the whisk attachment, beat the granulated sugar and oil for 6 minutes on high speed. Add the eggs 1 at a time and the egg white, combining well after each addition and scraping down the sides and bottom of the bowl as needed.

Turn your mixer down to its lowest speed and slowly add the flour and malt powder in 2 batches. Add the salt, baking powder, and baking soda. Be careful not to overbeat. Add the buttermilk and vanilla extract. Scrape down the sides and bottom of the bowl and mix until just combined. The finished batter should be pale yellow and have a silky texture.

Evenly pour the batter into the prepared pans. Bake for 25 to 30 minutes, or until a toothpick inserted into the center of a layer comes out just barely clean. It is crucial not to overbake this cake. The cake layers should have a rich golden color and a spongy texture with tiny bubbles.

Let the layers cool in the pans for 10 minutes, then invert onto wire racks. Let cool for 1 hour. Wrap each layer in plastic wrap and transfer to the freezer to chill for at least 2 hours.

FOR THE WHIPPED CREAM

Clean your stand mixer bowl and whisk attachment. Place them in the refrigerator for 15 minutes to get them nice and cold.

Remove the bowl and whisk attachment from the refrigerator. Add the heavy cream and whip on medium-high until soft peaks form.

Turn your mixer down to medium-low speed and add the confectioners' sugar and vanilla extract. Once the sugar is fully incorporated, turn your mixer speed back to high and continue to whip until stiff peaks form. Set aside.

TO ASSEMBLE

Warning: This process must move quickly.

Remove the cake layers from the freezer and unwrap them. Place one layer of cake in the center of your serving plate.

Remove 1 pan of ice cream from the freezer, unwrap it, and place the ice cream layer directly on top of the cake layer. Top the ice cream with the second cake layer.

Remove the second pan of ice cream from the freezer and top the second cake layer with the remaining ice cream. Top this with the final cake layer, bottom-side up.

Using an offset spatula, quickly spread the whipped cream on the outside of the cake. Smooth the whipped cream out with the spatula. Freeze until ready to serve. Use a warm knife to cut when serving. Store the cake in the freezer.

Grandbaby Notes: *This ice cream recipe makes about two quarts. If you have an ice cream maker with a lower capacity, just make it in two batches.*

For the cake, if you can't find malt powder, no worries. Just omit and increase your flour to three cups.

Ultimate Birthday Cake

SERVES 18-22

W HEN I WAS GROWING UP, I HAD SOME LEGENDARY BIRTHDAY PARTIES. FROM
Showbiz Pizza (this was pre–Chuck E. Cheese, for all the young'ns out there) to
McDonald's, complete with Ronald McDonald appearances and photo ops, I had some of
the world's best parties.

The birthday I remember the most is the one when I never even made it to my party. I
was turning seven. On the way to my shindig, my family got in a car accident that completely
totaled our car. Instead of being surrounded by balloons and confetti, we ended up at home re-
cuperating. A few days later, we celebrated my birthday with an ice cream cake in our kitchen.
I learned that no fuss is ever needed when you are surrounded by those who truly love you.
I still haven't outgrown the joy and excitement I get when it is time for my intimate birthday
dinner with just my mom, daddy, brother, and husband. It reminds me of the important things.

Here is a cake that is worth celebrating with, no matter how big or small your party.
Classic vanilla ice cream with sprinkles and cookie bits sandwiched between golden
sprinkle-filled cake layers is simply the best way to celebrate your special day. So, add your
candles to this masterpiece and make a wish. I know my wish is to always celebrate my
birthday with the ones I love.

INGREDIENTS

ICE CREAM

3	large eggs
2	large egg yolks
1½	cups granulated sugar
	Pinch salt
2	cups heavy cream
2	cups half-and-half
2	tablespoons vanilla extract
½	cup multicolored sprinkles
6	roughly-chopped cream-filled chocolate sandwich cookies, such as Oreos
6	roughly-chopped cream-filled vanilla sandwich cookies, such as Golden Oreos

CAKE

2½	cups granulated sugar
1½	cups vegetable oil
6	large eggs, room temperature
1	large egg white, room temperature
3	cups sifted all-purpose flour
1	teaspoon salt
½	teaspoon baking powder
½	teaspoon baking soda
1	cup buttermilk, room temperature
2	tablespoons vanilla extract
½	cup multicolored sprinkles

WHIPPED CREAM

3	cups heavy cream, cold
3	tablespoons confectioners' sugar
1	teaspoon vanilla extract
	Multicolored sprinkles, for garnish

FOR THE ICE CREAM

In a medium bowl, whisk together the eggs and egg yolks. Add the granulated sugar and salt and whisk to incorporate.

In a large saucepan over medium heat, bring the heavy cream and half-and-half to a boil. Once the mixture starts to boil, remove from the heat.

Slowly whisk 3 tablespoons of the hot heavy cream mixture into the egg mixture. Whisk constantly to make sure the eggs don't scramble and slowly add the rest of the heavy cream mixture. Stir in the vanilla extract. Refrigerate for 2 to 3 hours.

Remove from the refrigerator. Make ice cream according to your ice cream maker instructions.

While the ice cream churns, line 2 9-inch round cake pans with plastic wrap.

Once the ice cream is at the soft-serve stage, carefully fold in the sprinkles and cookies. Spoon the ice cream evenly into the prepared pans and cover the tops with more plastic wrap. Freeze for at least 5 hours, preferably overnight.

FOR THE CAKE

Preheat your oven to 325°F. Liberally prepare 3 9-inch round cake pans with the nonstick method of your choice. (I recommend the parchment method described on p. 17.)

In the bowl of your stand mixer fitted with the whisk attachment, beat the granulated sugar and oil on high speed for 6 minutes. Add the eggs 1 at a time and egg white, combining well after each addition and scraping down the sides and bottom of the bowl as needed.

Turn your mixer down to its lowest speed and slowly add the flour in 2 batches. Add the salt, baking powder, and baking soda. Be careful not to overbeat. Add the buttermilk and vanilla extract. Scrape down the sides and bottom of the bowl and mix until just combined. Be careful not to overmix. The finished batter should be pale yellow and have a silky texture. Carefully fold in the sprinkles.

Evenly pour the batter into the prepared pans. Bake for 25 to 30 minutes, or until a toothpick inserted into the center of a layer comes out just barely clean. It is crucial not to overbake this cake! The cake layers should have a rich golden color and a spongy texture with tiny bubbles.

Let the layers cool in the pans for 10 minutes, then invert them onto wire racks. Let cool for 1 hour. Wrap each layer in plastic wrap and freeze them for 2 hours.

FOR THE WHIPPED CREAM

Clean your stand mixer bowl and whisk attachment. Place them in the refrigerator for 15 minutes to get them nice and cold.

Remove the bowl and whisk attachment from the refrigerator. Add the heavy cream and whip on high speed until soft peaks begin to form.

Turn your mixer down to medium-low speed and slowly add the confectioners' sugar and vanilla extract. Once the sugar is fully incorporated, turn your mixer speed back to high and continue to whip until stiff peaks form. Set aside.

TO ASSEMBLE

Warning: This process must move quickly.

Remove the cake layers from the freezer and unwrap them. Place 1 layer of cake in the center of your serving plate.

Remove 1 pan of ice cream from the freezer, unwrap it, and place the ice cream layer directly on top of the cake layer. Top the ice cream with the second cake layer.

Remove the second pan of ice cream from the freezer and top the second cake layer with the remaining ice cream. Top this with the final cake layer, bottom-side up.

Using an offset spatula, quickly spread the outside of the cake with the whipped cream. Smooth the whipped cream out with the spatula. Decorate the cake with sprinkles. Freeze until ready to serve. Use a warm knife to cut when serving. Store the cake in the freezer.

Lighter Lemon Pound Cake

SERVES 12–16

T HIS IS MY ONE AND ONLY "LIGHTER" CAKE IN THIS COOKBOOK. THIS ISN'T because I hate anything that's good for me (though you might think otherwise; see Zucchini Cupcakes on p. 143); it's because I don't believe in having a dessert that isn't delicious, and many light recipes tend to taste bland. One exception is Patti LaBelle's *Lite Cuisine*. When I first bought that book I couldn't stop making her delicious, healthier recipes. And I loved the fact that I wasn't craving a cheeseburger after trying one. My Uncle Larry also eats pretty healthy and sticks to a very strict diet, so he has made me more conscious of the things I eat.

Big Daddy, Big Mama, and my Uncle Larry

This bright cake is not what you would call a diet recipe, but it might make you feel a bit better about having your dessert. It calls for fewer bad fats but still tastes delicious. It is moist and filled with the sweet fragrance and tart flavor of fresh lemon. The olive oil and Greek yogurt base perfectly balances out the citrus. A floral intensity from the olive oil adds a sophisticated undertone. It is indeed a grown folks' cake. As I have gotten older, I have learned to appreciate olive oil cakes. There is a level of refinement to their flavor that is truly for the mature palate. This is a very simple cake with simple flavors, but lightening up a traditional pound cake is cause enough for celebration in my book.

INGREDIENTS

CAKE

- 2 cups granulated sugar (or an appropriate amount of sugar substitute)
- 1¾ cups Greek yogurt, room temperature
- 6 large eggs, lightly beaten
- 1 cup extra virgin olive oil
- ¾ cup fresh lemon juice
- 1 tablespoon plus 1 teaspoon lemon zest
- 1 teaspoon lemon extract
- 1 teaspoon vanilla extract
- 3 cups sifted all-purpose flour
- 1 tablespoon baking powder
- 1 teaspoon salt

GLAZE

- 1 cup confectioners' sugar
- 3 tablespoons fresh lemon juice

FOR THE CAKE

Preheat your oven to 325°F. Prepare a 10-cup Bundt pan with the nonstick method of your choice.

In a large bowl, whisk together the granulated sugar, yogurt, eggs, oil, lemon juice, lemon zest, and lemon and vanilla extracts. Whisk in the flour 1 cup at a time, then whisk in the baking powder and salt. Mix until smooth, but be careful not to overmix.

Pour the batter into the prepared pan and bake for 70 to 80 minutes, or until a toothpick inserted into the center of the cake comes out mostly clean but still moist.

Let the cake cool in the pan for 10 minutes, then invert on a serving plate. Because of the oil, this cake should come out of the pan easily. Let cool to room temperature. Lightly cover the cake with foil or plastic wrap so it does not dry out.

FOR THE GLAZE

In a small bowl, whisk together the confectioners' sugar and lemon juice until smooth. Spoon over the cooled cake and serve.

Grandbaby Notes: *In addition to this cake being lighter, it is also easy to pull together. No mixer needed.*

To make this cake even lighter, try a sugar replacement of your choice and lose the glaze.

If you are not a fan of the stronger olive oil taste (and smell), you can replace it with a milder oil, like vegetable oil.

Sea Salt Caramel Cake

SERVES 18–22

THIS CAKE IS THE GROWN-UP VERSION OF THE REAL-DEAL CARAMEL CAKE (p. 65). Tender brown sugar cake layers are the ideal sponge for a perfectly sweet salted-caramel buttercream, which is then drizzled with salted caramel. If you love caramel but want some sophistication to your cake, this is seriously the recipe for you.

INGREDIENTS

CAKE

1 cup (2 sticks) unsalted butter, room temperature

2½ cups packed light brown sugar

7 large eggs, room temperature

3 cups sifted cake flour

1 teaspoon salt

½ teaspoon baking powder

½ teaspoon baking soda

1 cup buttermilk, room temperature

⅓ cup vegetable oil

2 tablespoons vanilla extract

SALTED-CARAMEL SAUCE

1 (12-ounce) can evaporated milk

1 cup granulated sugar

½ cup (1 stick) unsalted butter

1 teaspoon vanilla extract

1 teaspoon fine sea salt

Whole milk, for thinning the sauce (optional)

CARAMEL FROSTING

1 cup (2 sticks) unsalted butter, room temperature

4 ounces cream cheese, room temperature

4 cups confectioners' sugar

½ cup Salted-Caramel Sauce

1 tablespoon vanilla extract

¼ teaspoon fine sea salt

Caramel Shards (recipe follows) and coarse sea salt, for garnish

FOR THE CAKE

Preheat your oven to 325°F. Liberally prepare 3 9-inch round cake pans with the nonstick method of your choice. (I recommend the parchment method described on p. 17.)

In the bowl of your stand mixer fitted with the whisk attachment, beat the butter for 2 minutes on high speed. Slowly add the brown sugar. Cream together for an additional 5 minutes, until nice and fluffy. Add the eggs 1 at a time, combining well after each addition and scraping down the sides and bottom of the bowl as needed.

Turn your mixer down to its lowest speed and slowly add the flour in 2 batches. Add the salt, baking powder, and baking soda. Be careful not to overbeat. Pour in the buttermilk, oil, and vanilla extract. Scrape down the sides and bottom of the bowl and mix until just combined. Be careful not to overmix. The finished batter should have a silky texture.

Evenly pour the batter into the prepared pans and bake for 27 to 32 minutes, or until a toothpick inserted into the center of a layer comes out just barely clean. It is crucial not to overbake this cake. The layers should have a rich golden-brown color and a spongy texture.

Let the layers cool in the pans for 10 minutes, then invert onto wire racks. Let cool to room temperature for 1 hour. Lightly cover the cakes with foil or plastic wrap so they do not dry out.

FOR THE SALTED-CARAMEL SAUCE

In a medium saucepan over medium heat, melt the evaporated milk, granulated sugar, and butter. Continue to cook for 30 to 45 minutes, stirring frequently, until the caramel begins to boil and thicken. Keep watch on the saucepan, adjusting the heat to avoid burning the sauce. (See the Real-Deal Caramel Cake, p. 65, for more detailed instructions).

When the sauce can coat the back of a spoon, remove it from the heat and stir in the vanilla extract and salt. Let the sauce cool for about 6 to 8 minutes to let it thicken slightly.

Measure ½ cup of the sauce into a bowl and transfer to the refrigerator to cool. Set the rest of the caramel aside. If it gets too thick, whisk in some whole milk so that the sauce is thin enough to drizzle.

FOR THE CARAMEL FROSTING

Clean your stand mixer bowl and whisk attachment. Add the butter and cream cheese and beat on high speed for 2 minutes.

Turn your mixer down to low speed and slowly add the confectioners' sugar. Once the sugar is fully incorporated, turn your mixer speed back to high.

Remove the ½ cup of the caramel sauce from the refrigerator. Add it to your mixer, along with the vanilla extract and salt. Mix until the frosting is fluffy and smooth. Set aside.

TO ASSEMBLE

Once the layers are completely cooled, place 1 layer on a serving plate. Spread just the top with ⅓ of the frosting (please refer to the Basic Frosting Instructions on p. 18). Add the second layer and spread with ⅓ more of the frosting. Add the final layer, bottom-side up, and spread with the remaining frosting. Frost the top and the side of the cake.

Drizzle the remaining caramel sauce over the cake, allowing it to drip over the side. Garnish with the Caramel Shards and coarse sea salt. Serve at room temperature.

Grandbaby Note: *This cake can be quite tender. Chill the layers in the refrigerator for 20 to 30 minutes to firm them up before frosting.*

Caramel Shards

1   cup granulated sugar

½   cup water

½   teaspoon cream of tartar

Line a 9 × 11-inch baking sheet with nonstick aluminum foil.

In a small saucepan over medium-low heat, combine the ingredients. Cook until the sugar begins to caramelize and develops a light golden color, about 15 to 20 minutes. While the sugar cooks, use a wet pastry brush or cooking brush to melt any sugar crystals as they form on the side of the saucepan.

Remove from the heat and pour onto the prepared sheet, spreading the mixture out evenly. Let cool for 20 to 25 minutes. Break the caramel into uneven shards. Use as a garnish.

Snickers Cake

SERVES 18–22

GROWING UP WITH A DADDY WHO IS A DENTIST MEANT LOTS OF SNEAKING around for sweets. Cavities were no-nos, meaning candy was, too. Whenever I did actually indulge, it was always a Snickers bar out of any random (and well-hidden) vending machine after cheerleading or dance practice. Snickers was and continues to be the ultimate candy bar to me. Chewy peanut butter nougat, rich caramel, and salty peanuts wrapped in a chocolate package were just the cheat I needed.

Making a Snickers Cake was necessary for this chapter. It will remind you every bit of the candy bar, except the bottom is a moist and chocolaty sheet cake. Just when you thought a Snickers couldn't get better, I invented this to celebrate the fact that I'm an adult who doesn't have to sneak around anymore! I can have a Snickers Cake if I want to, when I want to (just don't tell my daddy, please).

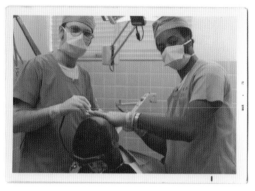

My daddy with his assistant during his early dentistry days

INGREDIENTS

CAKE
- ½ cup (1 stick) unsalted butter, room temperature
- ½ cup water
- ¼ cup vegetable oil
- 1 cup sifted all-purpose flour
- 1 cup granulated sugar
- 3 tablespoons unsweetened cocoa powder
- ½ teaspoon salt
- 1 large egg, room temperature
- ¼ cup buttermilk, room temperature
- ½ teaspoon baking soda

NOUGAT
- 4 tablespoons unsalted butter
- ¾ cup granulated sugar
- ⅓ cup evaporated milk
- 1⅔ cups marshmallow fluff
- ¼ cup smooth peanut butter
- 2 teaspoons vanilla extract

PEANUT-CARAMEL FILLING
- ½ cup (1 stick) unsalted butter
- 1 cup packed light brown sugar
- ½ cup heavy cream
- 1 cup roasted, salted peanuts, chopped
- 1 teaspoon vanilla extract
- Pinch salt

GANACHE
- 1 cup heavy cream
- 12 ounces bittersweet chocolate chips

FOR THE CAKE

Preheat your oven to 375°F. Prepare a 9 × 13-inch baking pan with the nonstick method of your choice. (I recommend the parchment method described on p. 17.)

In a medium saucepan over high heat, bring the butter, water, and oil to a boil. Once the mixture has melted and is starting to boil, remove from the heat and set aside.

In the bowl of your stand mixer fitted with the whisk attachment, mix together the flour, granulated sugar, cocoa powder, and salt on low speed.

Carefully add the hot butter mixture and increase the speed to medium. Add the egg and mix until well incorporated. Add the buttermilk and baking soda and mix the batter until just combined. Be careful not to overmix.

Pour the batter into prepared baking pan. Bake for 12 to 16 minutes, or until a toothpick inserted into the center of the cake comes out mostly clean but still moist. Let cool in the pan. Lightly cover the cake with foil or plastic wrap so it does not dry out. After it has cooled, put the cake in the refrigerator.

FOR THE NOUGAT

In a medium saucepan over medium-high heat, melt the butter. Whisk in the granulated sugar and evaporated milk until well incorporated. Allow the mixture to come to a boil for 3 minutes, then reduce the heat to low. Whisk in the marshmallow fluff, peanut butter, and vanilla extract until well incorporated. Remove from the heat. The mixture may look like a gooey mess, but this is perfectly normal.

Remove the cake from the refrigerator. Using a spatula, carefully pour the nougat over the cake and spread out the nougat evenly. Put the cake back in the refrigerator.

FOR THE PEANUT-CARAMEL FILLING

In a small saucepan over medium heat, melt the butter. Whisk in the brown sugar and bring to boil. Once the mixture begins to bubble, briskly whisk in the heavy cream and continue to whisk quickly until smooth. Continue to cook, allowing the mixture to bubble and thicken, until it coats the back of a spoon, about 10 minutes.

Once thick enough, remove from the heat and stir in the peanuts, vanilla extract, and salt.

Remove the cake from the refrigerator. Pour the filling over the nougat and spread out the filling evenly. Put the cake back in the refrigerator.

FOR THE GANACHE

In a medium saucepan over medium heat, melt the heavy cream and chocolate chips, whisking occasionally, until the mixture is smooth and shiny. Pour into another container, bring to room temperature, and refrigerate for 30 minutes to cool.

Once cool, remove the ganache and cake from the refrigerator. Pour the ganache over the cake. Let it set for 10 minutes, then freeze the cake for at least 1 hour, or until the nougat is firm. Serve chilled. Store the cake in the refrigerator.

Grandbaby Note: *You can also make the ganache in your microwave. Simply add the heavy cream and chocolate chips to a microwave-safe bowl and heat on high for 20-second intervals, whisking together after each heating until completely blended and smooth.*

Lava Flow Pound Cakelettes

MAKES 10–12

MY HUSBAND, FREDERICK, AND I GOT MARRIED ON THE HAWAIIAN ISLAND of Maui overlooking the Pacific Ocean. Not only were we fortunate to have over 60 family members and friends there to witness that magical day, my Big Daddy officiated our ceremony. When I think back on the beauty of that evening and how breathtaking everything was, I sometimes think it was all a dream. I still vividly remember the beautiful prayer my cousin Charley spoke. That day represented the union of two lives, two families, and new traditions I can't wait to pass down to my future children.

These cakelettes are a blend of the tropical flavors and influences we experienced during our two weeks on Maui and the Southern roots and heritage that shaped me (and my husband, coincidentally). The Lava Flow, a popular drink in Hawaii, is a fusion of piña colada and strawberry daiquiri flavors. The exquisite hints of coconut and pineapple throughout are only further enhanced by the lime- and rum-scented strawberry daiquiri syrup drizzled over them. In the end, they take the advice for "something old, something new" to a new level.

INGREDIENTS

PIÑA COLADA CAKELETTES

⅓ cup (5 tablespoons plus 1 teaspoon) unsalted butter, room temperature

1¼ cups granulated sugar

3 large eggs, room temperature

1⅓ cups sifted all-purpose flour

½ teaspoon salt

¼ teaspoon baking powder

¼ teaspoon baking soda

⅓ cup canned, no-sugar-added coconut milk

⅓ cup canned crushed pineapple, with juice

1 tablespoon vanilla extract

2 teaspoons vegetable oil

¼ teaspoon coconut extract

STRAWBERRY DAIQUIRI SYRUP

3 cups fresh strawberries, hulled and sliced

3 tablespoons rum

2 tablespoons granulated sugar

2 tablespoons fresh lime juice

FOR THE PIÑA COLADA CAKELETTES

Preheat your oven to 325°F. Prepare 2 5-cup mini Bundt pans with the nonstick method of your choice.

In the bowl of your stand mixer fitted with the whisk attachment, beat the butter for 2 minutes on high speed. Slowly add the sugar. Cream together for an additional 5 minutes, until very pale yellow and fluffy. Add the eggs 1 at a time, combining well after each addition and scraping down the sides and bottom of the bowl as needed.

Turn your mixer down to its lowest speed and slowly add the flour in 2 batches. Add the salt, baking powder, and baking soda. Be careful not to overbeat. Pour in the coconut milk, pineapple, vanilla extract, oil, and coconut extract. Scrape down the sides and bottom of the bowl and mix until just combined. Be careful not to overmix. The finished batter should be pale yellow and have a silky texture.

Using an ice cream scooper with a trigger release, scoop the batter into the prepared pans so that each cavity is ⅔ full. Be careful not to overfill. Bake for 20 to 24 minutes, or until a toothpick inserted into the center of a cakelette comes out just barely clean. Do not overbake!

Let the cakes cool for 10 minutes, then invert onto wire racks. Let cool to room temperature. Lightly cover the cakes with foil or plastic wrap so they do not dry out.

FOR THE STRAWBERRY DAIQUIRI SYRUP

In a small saucepan over medium-low heat, cook the strawberries, rum, sugar, and lime juice until the strawberries have softened and a syrup develops that is thick enough to coat the back of a spoon. Using a fork, mash the strawberries into the mixture and cook for another 2 to 3 minutes, until the syrup has thickened more. The liquid doesn't have to be perfectly smooth after this process.

Remove from the heat and strain through a fine-mesh strainer. Let cool for 15 to 20 minutes.

Using a toothpick or skewer, poke 2 or 3 holes into the top of each cakelette. Evenly drizzle the syrup over each cakelette. Serve at room temperature. Store the cakelettes in the refrigerator. Bring to room temperature before re-serving.

Fig–Brown Sugar Cake

SERVES 9

Big Mama is a fig expert. She has a towering fig tree in her backyard, which bears its earthy gifts in the late summer months. That reliable tree has quite the rich history in my family and has been bestowing its mysterious wonders to generation after generation. For decades, Big Mama has picked ripe, plump figs with bright-coral, syrupy centers from that tree, and each year when I come to visit, I can find rows and rows of her coveted fig preserves lining her cupboard, ready to be spread on her morning biscuits.

While most people know figs because of Fig Newtons from the grocery store, Big Mama knows them in their most intimate space, from the flesh of their pear-shaped outsides to the deep-honey intensity of their insides. It was only natural that I create a cake where Big Mama's figs could shine. By using fig preserves, you can make this simple and delightful cake any time of year (if figs aren't in season, you can make the cake without the garnish). The brown sugar and cinnamon are the figs' perfect companions. Simply put, this humble treat might just be the cake that does my family's lauded fig tree justice.

INGREDIENTS

CAKE

- ⅓ cup (5 tablespoons plus 1 teaspoon) unsalted butter, room temperature
- ¼ cup packed light brown sugar
- ¼ cup granulated sugar
- 1 large egg plus 1 large egg yolk, room temperature
- 1 cup sifted all-purpose flour
- 1 teaspoon baking powder
- ½ teaspoon salt
- ½ teaspoon ground cinnamon
- ¾ cup fig preserves
- ¼ cup sour cream, room temperature
- 2 teaspoons vanilla extract

HONEY-BUTTER DRIZZLE

- 2 tablespoons unsalted butter, melted
- 2 tablespoons honey
- 1 cup fresh fig halves, stems removed, for garnish

FOR THE CAKE

Preheat your oven to 350°F. Liberally prepare an 8 × 8-inch square cake pan with the nonstick method of your choice.

In the bowl of your stand mixer fitted with the whisk attachment, beat the butter for 1 minute on high speed. Slowly add both sugars. Cream together for an additional 5 minutes, until very golden yellow and fluffy. Add the egg and egg yolk 1 at a time, combining well after each addition and scraping down the sides and bottom of the bowl as needed.

Turn your mixer down to its lowest speed and slowly add the flour in 2 batches. Add the baking powder, salt, and cinnamon. Be careful not to overbeat. Add the fig preserves, sour cream, and vanilla extract. Scrape down the sides and bottom of the bowl and mix the batter until just combined. Be careful not to overmix.

Pour the batter into the prepared pan. Bake for 30 to 35 minutes, or until a toothpick inserted into the center of the cake comes out just barely clean. Do not overbake.

Let the cake cool in the pan for 10 minutes, then transfer to a serving plate. Let cool to room temperature. Lightly cover the cake with foil or plastic wrap so it does not dry out.

FOR THE HONEY–BUTTER DRIZZLE

In a small bowl, whisk together the melted butter and honey until well blended. Lightly drizzle ½ of this mixture over the cake.

Pile the fresh fig halves on top of the cake in a decorative pattern. Drizzle with the remaining honey–butter mixture. Serve.

CHAPTER 6

SEASONS
AND
HOLIDAYS

seasons AND holidays

WHEN THE CLOCK STRIKES MIDNIGHT ON JANUARY 1, we celebrate a new year filled with bright promise and potential. Our hearts swell with love as winter skates along, striking us with Cupid's arrow. Then spring and summer give way to bountiful fruit and charming breezes, along with Palm Sundays, Easter egg hunts, fireworks, and family barbecues. As the warm weather melts into the brisk days of fall and winter, our celebrations and holidays yield moments of graciousness and giving. These cakes celebrate a full year of the seasons and holidays we cherish the most. They remind us that the foundation of those festivities is family. For me, it isn't the gorgeous Christmas tree or the Cajun fried turkey that means the most (though they are still quite awesome). The moments of sitting around the beautifully decorated dining room table listening to my family's knee-slapping tales or pearls of wisdom linger just as long as the first taste of one of Big Mama's masterpiece cakes. I can still hear the echoes of laughter and can feel the life in our home.

I hope you will not only share one of these cakes on your favorite holiday, but hop in the kitchen with a family member and bake one together. I can't tell you how many memories I have in the kitchen on Thanksgiving that I will hold dear for the rest of my life.

Blood-Orange Mimosa Cake

SERVES 12–16

U NCLE SONNY, BIG MAMA'S FIRSTBORN AND MY MOM'S OLDER BROTHER, WAS
the life of the party, and the truth is, he didn't have to try hard. He just knew how to
have a good time. His electric energy, sense of humor, smooth walk, and fly metallic suits
were quite the sight to behold, and to talk to him was to have an "experience." Visits to
Uncle Sonny, who lived in Flint, Michigan, were so
exciting, and we always had a good time.

This cake immediately calls Uncle Sonny to mind.
He truly loved his bubbly, but that's not why this cake is
appropriate. With its hints of crisp, pink champagne and
distinctive blood-orange juice, this is a statement cake,
which makes it perfect for any New Year's Eve party.

Blood oranges are available only during a small
window of time, making them really special. In fact,
you learn to appreciate them all the more because of
this. When Uncle Sonny passed away a few years ago, I
realized how one of a kind he truly was.

Grandbaby Note: *You can use any orange you want in
this recipe if blood oranges are not in season. The cake is
quite versatile.*

INGREDIENTS

CAKE

1½ cups (3 sticks) unsalted butter, room
temperature

2¾ cups granulated sugar

5 large eggs, room temperature

3 cups sifted cake flour

½ teaspoon salt

1 cup pink Moscato or Champagne

3 tablespoons orange zest

1 tablespoon vanilla extract

SIMPLE SYRUP

½ cup pink Moscato or Champagne

½ cup granulated sugar

¼ cup fresh blood-orange juice

ORANGE GLAZE

1½ cups confectioners' sugar

3 tablespoons fresh blood-orange juice

FOR THE CAKE

Preheat your oven to 315°F. Liberally prepare a 10-cup Bundt pan with the nonstick method of your choice.

In the bowl of your stand mixer fitted with the whisk attachment, beat the butter for 2 minutes on high speed. Slowly add the granulated sugar. Cream together for an additional 5 minutes, until very pale yellow and fluffy. Add the eggs 1 at a time, combining well after each addition and scraping down the sides and bottom of the bowl as needed.

Turn your mixer down to its lowest speed and slowly add the flour in 2 batches. Add the salt. Be careful not to overbeat. Add the Moscato, orange zest, and vanilla extract. Scrape down the sides and bottom of the bowl and mix the batter until just combined. Be careful not to overmix.

Pour the batter into the prepared pan. Bake for 70 to 80 minutes, or until a toothpick inserted into the center of the cake comes out clean.

Let the cake cool in the pan for 10 minutes, then invert onto a wire rack. Let cool to room temperature. Lightly cover the cake with foil or plastic wrap so it does not dry out.

FOR THE SIMPLE SYRUP

In a small pot over medium-high heat, combine the Moscato, granulated sugar, and orange juice. Once the liquid has reduced by ⅓ and thickened, cook for about 5 minutes. Remove from the heat and set aside to cool.

FOR THE ORANGE GLAZE

In a medium bowl, whisk the confectioners' sugar and orange juice together until smooth and thick but still pourable. Set aside.

TO ASSEMBLE

Liberally poke the top of the cake with a toothpick or skewer, then pour the syrup in intervals over the entire cake, letting it seep in each time before adding more, until all the syrup is gone. There is a lot of syrup, but the cake is quite delicious when soaked through. If you don't want to add all the syrup, that is also fine.

Drizzle the glaze over the cake. Let the glaze set for 10 minutes. Serve at room temperature.

Strawberry "Eat Your Heart Out" Cake

MAKES 2 6-INCH CAKES OR 1 9- OR 10-INCH CAKE

W HEN I WAS GROWING UP, EVERY YEAR FOR VALENTINE'S DAY MY MOM AND I
would make a giant (I'm talking huge), heart-shaped, pink strawberry cake with
darling bubblegum-pink frosting. To do this, we'd bake one round cake and one square cake,
cut the round in half, and place the two halves
on adjacent sides of the square layer. The love
and memories of baking with my mom always
made the holiday much more special for me.

Now that I'm older, I love making this version, which is more refined than my childhood
heart-shaped cake. This berry-scented, blush-
colored cake crowned by crimson strawberry
slices is definitely worthy of sharing with your
sweetheart. But for me, this cake is dedicated
to my loving Mommy. She will always be my
number one valentine.

*Grandbaby Note: This recipe uses a specialty heart pan. Fat Daddio's has a great 6-inch one
that is quite reasonable. However, you can use one 9- or 10-inch round pan to bake one cake. Just
watch the baking time, as it will take a few minutes more to bake completely through.*

INGREDIENTS

STRAWBERRY TOPPING

¼ cup granulated sugar

8 fresh medium-sized strawberries,
   hulled and sliced

CAKE

¾ cup granulated sugar

⅓ cup (5 tablespoons plus 1 teaspoon)
   unsalted butter, room temperature

½ cup strawberry purée (whole
   strawberries puréed in a food processor)

1 large egg, room temperature

1 large egg yolk, room temperature

1½ cups sifted all-purpose flour

½ teaspoon baking powder

½ teaspoon baking soda

½ teaspoon salt

⅓ cup sour cream

¼ cup vegetable oil

1 teaspoon strawberry extract

½ teaspoon vanilla extract

GARNISH

4 coffee stirrers

2 fresh medium-sized strawberries,
   hulled and halved

   Confectioners' sugar, for sprinkling

FOR THE STRAWBERRY TOPPING

Preheat your oven to 350° F. Liberally prepare 2 6 × 2-inch heart-shaped pans with nonstick baking spray. Cut a piece of parchment paper to fit each pan and use it to line the bottoms. Spray the parchment paper with the nonstick spray. Sprinkle granulated sugar over the parchment paper.

Arrange the sliced strawberries in the pans, covering the entire surface. Set the pans aside.

FOR THE CAKE

In the bowl of your stand mixer fitted with the whisk attachment, cream together the butter and granulated sugar for 5 minutes on high speed. Add the strawberry purée, egg, and egg yolk, combining well after each addition and scraping down the sides and bottom of the bowl as needed.

Turn your mixer down to low speed and add the flour, baking powder, baking soda, and salt. Be careful not to overbeat. Add the sour cream, oil, and strawberry and vanilla extracts. Scrape down the sides and bottom of the bowl and mix the batter until just combined. Be careful not to overmix.

Evenly pour the batter into the prepared pans, over the strawberries. Bake for 30 to 35 minutes, or until a toothpick inserted into the center of a cake comes out clean.

Let the cakes cool in the pans for 6 minutes, then run a knife along the edge and turn each cake out onto a separate serving plate. Remove and discard the parchment paper.

FOR THE GARNISH

Push a coffee stirrer through the side of 1 of the cakes, on an angle. Push a second stirrer through the opposite side, to make it look like the stirrer is running all the way through the cake. Pierce 1 strawberry half, face up, with the stirrer on the lower side of the heart cake. Pierce a second strawberry half, face down, with the stirrer on the higher side of the heart cake. Repeat with the second cake.

Sprinkle the cakes with the confectioners' sugar. Serve warm.

Mango Swirl Carrot Cake

SERVES 20-24

Carrots' vibrant colors can be so entrancing. Gathered from the earth, their shades range from radiant saffron and orange to intense violet, and their tops sprout full heads of green hair.

Carrots weren't my favorite vegetable growing up (like I've said before, I wasn't a fan of most veggies—see Zucchini Cupcakes on p. 143), but I did love them in classic carrot cake. My Auntie Rose makes a wonderful carrot cake that debuts every spring on Easter Sunday. Three regally tall layers of perfectly spiced cake are draped in cream cheese frosting. There is always a space in my heart for the classic, but something about this version is so unique and really kind of cool. The cake starts with a traditional carrot batter, but I've infused it with the warmth of aromatic spices and mango undertones. The top is killer. You don't have to frost this cake, because the frosting is baked right in. Swirls of mango-infused cream cheese create a visual stunner in an otherwise unfussy cake. Easter just got easier, and a bit tastier, too.

Grandbaby Note: To cut a mango, simply halve the mango, then cut several vertical and then horizontal parallel lines into each half, resulting in a checkerboard look. Then either scoop the sliced mango out with a spoon or cut it out. You can also defrost some frozen mango pieces to save time.

INGREDIENTS

CAKE

1¾	cups granulated sugar
12	ounces freshly grated carrots
4	large eggs, room temperature
½	cup mango-flavored Greek yogurt, room temperature
½	cup vegetable oil
1	tablespoon vanilla extract
2¼	cups all-purpose flour
2	teaspoons baking powder
2	teaspoons ground cinnamon
1	teaspoon salt

¼	teaspoon baking soda
¼	teaspoon ground cloves
¼	teaspoon freshly ground nutmeg

CREAM CHEESE SWIRL

1	(8-ounce) package cream cheese, room temperature
¼	cup plus 2 tablespoons granulated sugar
1	large egg, room temperature
3	tablespoons mango purée (fresh mango puréed in a food processor until smooth)
1	teaspoon vanilla extract

FOR THE CAKE

Preheat your oven to 375°F. Prepare a 9 × 13-inch baking pan with the nonstick method of your choice. (I recommend the parchment method described on p. 17.)

In a large bowl, combine the sugar, carrots, eggs, yogurt, oil, and vanilla extract.

In a separate bowl, sift together the flour, baking powder, cinnamon, salt, baking soda, cloves, and nutmeg.

Slowly add the dry ingredients to the wet ingredients and whisk until well incorporated. Set aside.

FOR THE CREAM CHEESE SWIRL

In a medium bowl, beat the cream cheese and sugar with a hand mixer until nice and smooth. Add the egg, mango purée, and vanilla extract and mix until well incorporated. Set aside.

TO ASSEMBLE

Pour ¾ of the batter into the prepared pan. Evenly spread the cream cheese mixture on top of the batter, until the batter is completely hidden. Spoon the remaining batter in random areas over the cream cheese mixture.

Using a butter knife or skewer, create a swirl pattern in the batter. Bake for 40 to 50 minutes, or until a toothpick inserted into the center of the cake comes out clean.

Let cool to room temperature. Lightly cover the cake with foil or plastic wrap so it does not dry out. Store the cake in the refrigerator. Remove from the refrigerator 15 to 20 minutes before serving.

Watermelon-Berry-Lime Icebox Cake

SERVES 8

MY MOTHER AND AUNT ARE BOTH LADIES OF ALPHA KAPPA ALPHA SORORITY, Inc., so it was inevitable that I would become one, too. The grace, the intelligence, the class, and the sisterly love were all I heard about growing up. I reveled in listening to the old Tougaloo College tales of Greek step shows, 20 pearls, community service and civil rights activism, and Founders' Days.

When I thought about dedicating a cake to my dear AKA, the luminous watermelon came to mind. It sparkles with its apple-green exterior, encasing salmon-pink sweet flesh, the colors of my sorority. In this fun cake, the delicious flavor of watermelon is undeniable, especially when paired with tart lime and the sweetness of berries. So when summer finally arrives and watermelons make their debut, pick some up to refresh yourself as the sweltering heat unpacks itself and stays a spell. This no-bake cake is as cooling as it is delightful, and it is the perfect compromise for those who still crave down-home delights in the heat. If there were ever a cake that was perfectly sisterly, it would be this one. I dedicate it to my sorors.

Grandbaby Notes: *This is a fun recipe that you can really play with according to your fruit preferences. Try more strawberry, more watermelon, or all of one. Heck, try other berries and summer fruit blends that you love. Playing it by ear is pretty safe with an icebox cake.*

Feel free to fluctuate the sugar amount to your preference. It will really depend on the sweetness of your fruit.

Mom, me, and Auntie Rose

1½ cups chopped seedless watermelon

1½ cups strawberries, hulled

2 cups heavy cream, cold

1 (8-ounce) package cream cheese, room temperature

½–¾ cup granulated sugar (depending on the sweetness of the fruit)

2 teaspoons lime zest, plus more for garnish

Pinch salt

3–8 drops red food coloring (optional)

12 graham cracker rectangles (keep in large pieces; do not break apart)

In a food processor or heavy-duty blender, purée the watermelon and strawberries until smooth. Using a fine-mesh strainer, strain the juice. Reserve ½ cup of the pulp and 2 to 3 tablespoons of the juice.

In the bowl of your stand mixer fitted with the whisk attachment, beat the heavy cream, cream cheese, and sugar on low speed until incorporated.

Turn your mixer up to medium-high speed and beat until soft peaks form. Add the reserved pulp and juice, lime zest, and salt. If using red food coloring, add drops until the color is to your liking. Continue to mix until stiff peaks form. Refrigerate this cream filling for 1 hour, to stiffen.

In a springform pan, arrange 2 graham crackers side by side vertically.

Remove the cream filling from the refrigerator and transfer it into a piping bag with a No. 12 round tip (or similar), or quart-sized resealable plastic bag with a corner cut off. (You can also just use an offset spatula for a less precise, more rustic look.)

Pipe ⅙ of the cream on top of first graham crackers, then arrange 2 more graham crackers on top of the filling horizontally. Pipe ⅙ of the cream on top of the graham crackers. Repeat this step, alternating the graham crackers in rows of horizontal and vertical, until you have the 6th and final layer of graham crackers. Pipe side-by-side dots of cream on top of this last layer.

Refrigerate for at least 6 hours, preferably overnight, to soften the graham crackers. Garnish with the lime zest before serving. Serve cold.

Arnold Palmer Cake

SERVES 18–22

W HEN I THINK OF A CALM AND RELAXING DAY, I IMMEDIATELY IMAGINE sitting in a rocking chair in the South, sipping sweet tea. This daydream is a far cry from the reality of my daily life in the temperamental weather of the Windy City. Sweet tea has always been the drink of the South, recognizable by its amber-toned brew and deep flavor balanced by the hints of lemon and sweetness that only heaps of sugar can provide. I know whenever I visit my Big Mama we are sure to have a pitcher of it on the dinner table.

While Big Mama is mostly a sweet-tea woman, I was also a fan of homemade lemonade when I was growing up. That is one reason why good ol'-fashioned Arnold Palmers (half iced tea and half lemonade) were like an angel from God when I first discovered them. This recipe is an ode to the drink that solved my *what do I fill my mason jar with?* conundrum, perfectly melding both flavors in the most delightful cake. The lemon cake might make you pucker, and its topping of smooth sweet-tea buttercream, steeped with Lipton or Luzianne tea, is sure to make you wonder how you can put it in a cup and drink it. When I took my first bite, I felt like I was back in Mississippi on my Big Mama's porch instead of in the harsh weather realities of Chicago.

INGREDIENTS

LEMONADE CAKE

1   cup (2 sticks) unsalted butter, room temperature

2½ cups granulated sugar

4   large eggs, room temperature

3   cups sifted all-purpose flour

2½ teaspoons baking powder

1½ teaspoons salt

⅔   cup sour cream, room temperature

2   tablespoons fresh lemon juice

2   tablespoons vegetable oil

1½ teaspoons lemon oil or 6 tablespoons lemon zest

1   teaspoon vanilla extract

SWEET-TEA BUTTERCREAM

4   bags black Lipton or Luzianne tea

½   cup boiling water

2   cups (4 sticks) unsalted butter, room temperature

6   cups confectioners' sugar

1   teaspoon lemon extract

    Lemon slices and mint leaves, for garnish

FOR THE CAKE

Preheat your oven to 350°F. Liberally prepare 3 9-inch round cake pans with the nonstick method of your choice. (I recommend the parchment method described on p. 17; these layers have a tendency to stick.)

In the bowl of your stand mixer fitted with the whisk attachment, beat the butter for 2 minutes on high speed. Slowly add the granulated sugar. Cream together for an additional 5 minutes, until very pale yellow and fluffy. Add the eggs 1 at a time, combining well after each addition and scraping down the sides and bottom of the bowl as needed.

Turn your mixer down to its lowest speed and slowly add the flour in 2 batches. Add the baking powder and salt. Be careful not to overbeat. Add the sour cream, lemon juice, vegetable oil, lemon oil, and vanilla extract. Scrape down the sides and bottom of the bowl and mix until just combined. Be careful not to overmix. The finished batter should be pale yellow and have a silky texture.

Evenly pour the batter into the prepared pans and bake for 22 to 28 minutes, or until a toothpick inserted into the center of a layer comes out just barely clean. Do not overbake. The layers should have a rich golden color and spongy texture, with tiny bubbles on top.

Let the layers cool in the pans for 10 minutes, then invert onto wire racks. Let cool for 1 hour. Lightly cover the layers with foil or plastic wrap so they do not dry out.

FOR THE SWEET-TEA BUTTERCREAM

Place the tea bags in the boiling water and steep for 45 minutes. Remove the bags, squeezing all the water from them. Discard the tea bags. Refrigerate the tea for 30 minutes.

Clean your stand mixer bowl and whisk attachment. Beat the butter for 2 minutes on high speed. Add the tea and mix to combine.

Turn your mixer down to low speed and slowly add the confectioners' sugar. Once the sugar is fully incorporated, turn your mixer speed back to high. Add the lemon extract and whip until the frosting is fluffy and smooth. Set aside.

TO ASSEMBLE

Once the layers are completely cooled, place 1 layer on a serving plate. Spread just the top of the layer with ⅓ of the frosting (please refer to the Basic Frosting Instructions on p. 18). Add the second layer and spread with another ⅓ of the frosting. Add the final layer, bottom-side up, and spread with the remaining frosting. Frost the top and the side of the cake. Garnish with the lemon slices and mint leaves. Serve at room temperature.

Grandbaby Note: *Lemon oil is a great time-saving product because you don't have to grate a bunch of zest, which is needed to make this cake really citrusy. However, if you don't have access to the oil, you can still make this cake by substituting the lemon oil with six tablespoons of lemon zest, which takes about four to six lemons, depending on their size.*

Caramel-Apple Pound Cakelettes

MAKES 6-8

T HE FIRST DAYS OF AUTUMN ARE ALWAYS SO COMFORTING, LIKE A BLANKET that's worn and cozy from supporting several years of naps. As the season is fully realized, the delicate summer breeze grows edgier and the trees awaken with warm electrifying tones. In the country, you may find some of those trees dripping with a harvest of inviting green and red apples, ripe for picking and filling pies and Dutch babies. Personally, I love to dunk them in a sea of Aunt Beverly's silky caramel for a classic taffy-apple treat.

These cakelettes are the perfect Southern rendition of that classic fall delight. Their petite size and dainty shape mimic the round fruit, and their crown of sautéed apple slices and caramel sauce, complete with charming little stems, will give you just the caramel-apple taste you long for during autumn—but with some Southern charm, of course.

INGREDIENTS

CAKELETTES

¾ cup (1½ sticks) unsalted butter, room temperature
4 ounces cream cheese, room temperature
1 tablespoon shortening
1⅓ cups granulated sugar
3 large eggs, room temperature
1½ cups sifted cake flour
2 teaspoons vanilla extract
½ teaspoon salt

SAUTÉED APPLES

2 tablespoons unsalted butter
¾ teaspoon fresh lemon juice

¼ cup granulated sugar
2 Granny Smith apples, peeled and thinly sliced
1 tablespoon heavy cream
1 tablespoon rum
½ teaspoon vanilla extract
½ teaspoon ground cinnamon

CARAMEL ICING AND ASSEMBLY

¾ cup evaporated milk
½ cup granulated sugar
2 tablespoons unsalted butter
½ teaspoon vanilla extract
   Pinch salt
6-8 small pretzel sticks

FOR THE CAKE

Preheat your oven to 325°F. Liberally prepare 2 5-cup or 6-cup mini Bundt pans with the nonstick method of your choice.

In the bowl of your stand mixer fitted with the whisk attachment, beat the butter, cream cheese, and shortening for 2 minutes on high speed. Slowly add the sugar. Cream together for an additional 5 minutes, until very pale yellow and fluffy. Add the eggs 1 at a time, combining well after each addition and scraping down the sides and bottom of the bowl as needed.

Turn your mixer down to its lowest speed and slowly add the flour. Add the vanilla extract and salt. Be careful not to overbeat. Scrape down the sides and bottom of the bowl and mix the batter until just combined. Be careful not to overmix.

Using an ice cream scooper with a trigger release, scoop the batter into the prepared pans until each cavity is ¾ full. Be careful not to overfill. Bake for 20 to 25 minutes, or until a toothpick inserted into the center of a cakelette comes out just barely clean. Do not overbake.

Let the cakelettes cool in the pan for 10 minutes, then invert onto wire racks. Let cool to room temperature. Lightly cover the cakelettes with foil or plastic wrap so they do not dry out.

FOR THE SAUTÉED APPLES

In a medium sauté pan over low heat, melt the butter and lemon. Whisk in the sugar and increase the heat to medium. Watch until the mixture begins to turn a caramel-brown color, which can take up to 8 minutes. Make sure the mixture does not burn.

Add the apple slices, heavy cream, rum, vanilla extract, and cinnamon and cook until tender, about 10 to 12 minutes. While the apples sauté, start the caramel icing. When the apples are tender, remove from the heat and set aside to cool for 10 minutes.

FOR THE CARAMEL ICING

In a medium saucepan over medium heat, add the evaporated milk, sugar, and butter. Reduce the heat to medium-low and cook for 25 to 30 minutes, stirring frequently, until the caramel begins to boil and thicken. Keep close watch, adjusting the heat to avoid burning.

Remove from the heat, add the vanilla extract and salt, and let cool for about 6 to 8 minutes to slightly thicken.

TO ASSEMBLE

Carefully spoon the sautéed apples on top of each cakelette. Drizzle caramel icing over the apples. Insert a pretzel stick into the center of each cakelette to resemble an apple stem. Serve at room temperature.

Coffee-Toffee Pumpkin Cupcakes

MAKES 18-20

P UMPKIN NEVER MADE AN APPEARANCE IN MY BAKING UNTIL ADULTHOOD. That's because my truly Southern family is loyally devoted to the sweet potato and all its glory. There is nothing quite like the spicy aroma of a sweet potato pie baking in the oven on Thanksgiving. Like a good girl, I followed suit and steered clear of pumpkin, until the day a friend convinced me to try pumpkin ice cream. That was the moment, nearly 10 years ago, that the affair began, and my heart has been torn ever since.

The truth is, I can't imagine an autumn without both flavors coexisting in my menu lineup. Jazz either one up with cinnamon, nutmeg, and other copper-colored spices, and you are looking at the most fantastically warm flavors that fall can offer. This cupcake recipe in particular is a superb cheat for those married to sweet potato. Each cupcake is perfectly spiced, moist, and tender with a cream cheese buttercream spiked with coffee and infused with brown sugar. I invented this recipe to lure my family away from its all-or-nothing allegiance—just a teeny bit. When they took a bite, it was if these cupcakes gently whispered, "Can't we all just get along?"

INGREDIENTS

CUPCAKES

2	large eggs, room temperature
½	cup granulated sugar
¼	cup packed light brown sugar
1	cup canned pumpkin
½	cup vegetable oil
¼	cup hot water
1	teaspoon instant coffee powder
1	cup sifted all-purpose flour
1	teaspoon baking powder powder
1	teaspoon salt
1	teaspoon ground cinnamon
½	teaspoon baking soda
¼	teaspoon ground nutmeg
¼	teaspoon ground cloves

SPICED BUTTERCREAM

1½	cups confectioners' sugar
1	cup (2 sticks) unsalted butter, room temperature
6	ounces cream cheese, room temperature
2	tablespoons heavy cream, cold
2	teaspoons vanilla extract
½	teaspoon ground cinnamon
¼	teaspoon instant coffee powder
¼	teaspoon ground nutmeg
	Pinch salt

TOFFEE SAUCE

⅔	cup packed light brown sugar
½	cup (1 stick) unsalted butter
¼	cup heavy cream, plus more to thin out the sauce if needed
½	teaspoon cornstarch

FOR THE CUPCAKES

Preheat your oven to 350°F. Line 2 12-well muffin pans with 18 to 20 cupcake liners.

In the bowl of your stand mixer fitted with the whisk attachment, beat the eggs, granulated sugar, and brown sugar for 3 minutes on high speed. Add the pumpkin, oil, hot water, and instant coffee and mix until incorporated. Scrape the side and bottom of the bowl as needed.

Turn your mixer down to its lowest speed and carefully add the flour, baking powder, salt, cinnamon, baking soda, nutmeg, and cloves. Mix the batter until just combined. Do not overmix.

Using an ice cream scooper with a trigger release, scoop the batter into the cupcake liners until each is ⅔ full. Be careful not to overfill. Bake for 16 to 20 minutes, or until a toothpick inserted into the center of a cupcake comes out barely clean.

Let the cupcakes cool in the pans for 10 minutes, then transfer to wire racks. Let cool to room temperature. Lightly cover the cupcakes with foil or plastic wrap so they do not dry out.

FOR THE SPICED BUTTERCREAM

Clean your stand mixer bowl and whisk attachment. Combine the confectioners' sugar, butter, and cream cheese on low speed.

When the mixture has just come together, increase your mixer speed to high and mix for another 2 minutes. Add the heavy cream, vanilla extract, cinnamon, instant coffee, nutmeg, and salt and continue to mix until the buttercream is fluffy. Refrigerate for 20 to 30 minutes to firm up.

When the buttercream is firm and the cupcakes are room temperature, frost the cupcakes.

FOR THE TOFFEE SAUCE

In a small saucepan over medium heat, whisk together the brown sugar and butter. Bring to a boil, then quickly whisk in the heavy cream until it is completely incorporated and the mixture has settled. Keep the mixture at a boil until it has thickened slightly, about 2 to 3 minutes, whisking occasionally.

Remove from the heat and whisk in the cornstarch. Whisk until the sauce is smooth, then set aside to cool to room temperature. Don't allow this to cool too long, or it will get a bit too thick to drizzle. If this does happen, just add 1 to 2 teaspoons of heavy cream to the sauce and whisk to thin it out some. The mixture should coat the back of a spoon but quickly slide off.

Drizzle the sauce over the frosted cupcakes. Serve at room temperature.

Grandbaby Note: *You will have leftover pumpkin from this recipe. I love to use it in other recipes: french toast, oatmeal, and even morning smoothies! Just make sure you keep it refrigerated and use it within four to five days of opening.*

*Mama Ramey (Uncle BB's mother)
and Uncle Larry (my mom's brother)*

Merry Berry Christmas Cake

SERVES 20–24

WINTER CAN BE SO ENCHANTING WITH ITS MILKY SNOWFLAKES, AND THE slower pace really lets you soak in the Christmas moments. With each passing year, my priorities shift more and more from the things underneath the tree to the memories I can treasure, hold on to, and look back fondly on. A crackling fireplace; quality time with all of my family, including my Uncles Sidney, Larry, Terry, and BB; Donny Hathaway's "This Christmas" playing in the background; a family game of Taboo (which can get quite competitive); and a slice of this festive cake are all I need around that time of year.

This Merry Berry Christmas Cake is all about cherishing and indulging in those memories. It's a perfect holiday cake, and I plan to open presents every year while eating a nice big slice of it.

Grandbaby Notes: *To melt the raspberry jam, place it in a microwave-safe bowl and heat on high for 20 to 30 seconds until it is runny and thinned.*

To catch any juices that may drip while the cake bakes, add a sheet of parchment paper or foil on a shelf below the Bundt pan.

Uncle Terry (my mom's youngest brother) and Auntie Rose

INGREDIENTS

BERRY TOP

- 3 tablespoons unsalted butter, melted
- 1 cup packed light brown sugar, divided
- ¼ teaspoon ground cinnamon
- 1¼ cups fresh raspberries
- 1¼ cups fresh cranberries

CAKE

- 1½ cups (3 sticks) unsalted butter, room temperature
- 2¾ cups granulated sugar
- 6 large eggs, room temperature

- 3 cups sifted all-purpose flour
- 1¼ teaspoons ground cinnamon
- 1 teaspoon salt
- 1 cup sour cream, room temperature
- 1 tablespoon vanilla extract
  Confectioners' sugar for dusting (optional)

SWIRL

- 3 tablespoons seedless raspberry jam, melted
- 3–4 drops red food coloring

FOR THE TOP

Preheat your oven to 325°F. Prepare a 12-cup Bundt pan with the nonstick method of your choice.

Add the melted butter to bottom of the Bundt pan. Cover the butter with ¾ cup of the brown sugar and the cinnamon.

Evenly spread the raspberries and cranberries over the brown sugar, covering the entire area. Carefully pat down the berries inside the pan.

Cover the berries with the remaining ¼ cup of brown sugar. Set aside.

FOR THE CAKE

In the bowl of your stand mixer fitted with the whisk attachment, add the butter and beat on high speed for 1 minute. Slowly add the granulated sugar. Cream together for an additional 5 minutes, until very pale yellow and fluffy. Add the eggs 1 at a time, combining well after each addition and scraping down the sides and bottom of the bowl as needed.

In a separate medium bowl, whisk together the flour, cinnamon, and salt. Turn your mixer down to its lowest speed and slowly add the flour mixture in 2 batches. Be careful not to over-beat. Add the sour cream and vanilla extract. Scrape down the sides and bottom of the bowl and mix the batter until just combined. Be careful not to overmix.

FOR THE SWIRL

Remove 1 cup of the batter from the mixing bowl and add it to a separate small bowl.

Stir in the melted raspberry jam and red food coloring and whisk until smooth. Set aside.

TO ASSEMBLE

Evenly pour ⅓ of the plain batter into the Bundt pan over the berries. Add ½ of the swirl batter on top. Add another ⅓ of the plain batter and the remaining swirl batter on top. Then add the remaining ⅓ of the plain batter on top.

Bake for 1 hour and 15 to 25 minutes, or until a toothpick inserted into the top of cake comes out clean.

Remove the cake from the oven. Let cool for only 5 to 7 minutes, then carefully invert the cake onto a wire rack to finish cooling. If any berries stick to the pan, carefully use a butter knife to remove them and place them back on top of the cake. Lightly cover the cake with foil or plastic wrap so it does not dry out. Let the juices settle (to speed this process, you can refrigerate).

If using, garnish with a small sprinkling of confectioners' sugar. Serve at room temperature.

Red Velvet S'more Cake

SERVES 18-22

CHRISTMASTIME IS A BIG DEAL IN MY FAMily. We not only celebrate the birth of Christ with a huge affair, we also celebrate my cousin Roslynn's birthday, complete with balloons, presents, and birthday cake. A few years back, I made a beautiful red velvet cake to celebrate, and that cake hasn't been forgotten.

Red velvet has already made an appearance in this cookbook, but this is the ultimate. Can you imagine the smokiness and gooeyness of s'mores paired with red velvet? This is the perfect masterpiece to serve on Christmas Day. The beautiful ruby-red layers, baked on a graham cracker crust and blanketed in toasty marshmallow fluff like a delicate snowfall, are as delightful as humanly possible. This will inspire *oohs* and *aahs* without a doubt, so allow it to be the centerpiece around which laughter and family connections are built. If this cake does anything for you, I hope it inspires new memories to cherish this holiday season.

My cousin Roslynn celebrating her 3rd birthday on Christmas day.

INGREDIENTS

GRAHAM CRACKER CRUST

- 3 cups graham cracker crumbs
- ½ cup plus 2 tablespoons (1¼ sticks) unsalted butter, melted
- ⅓ cup granulated sugar

CAKE

- 2½ cups sifted all-purpose flour
- 2 cups granulated sugar
- 2 tablespoons unsweetened cocoa powder
- 1 teaspoon baking soda
- 1 teaspoon salt
- 1⅓ cups vegetable oil
- 1 cup buttermilk, room temperature
- 2 large eggs, room temperature
- ¼ cup strong coffee, hot
- 1 ounce liquid red food coloring
- 1 tablespoon vanilla extract
- 1 teaspoon apple cider vinegar

MARSHMALLOW FLUFF

- 7 large egg whites, room temperature
- 1½ cups granulated sugar
- 6 tablespoons light corn syrup
- 1 teaspoon vanilla extract

FOR THE GRAHAM CRACKER CRUST

Preheat your oven to 350°F. Prepare 3 9-inch round cake pans with the nonstick method of your choice. (I recommend the parchment method described on p. 17.)

In a medium bowl, whisk the ingredients together until moist.

Divide the graham cracker mixture evenly among 2 of the prepared pans. Pat down into the bottoms and set aside.

FOR THE CAKE

In the bowl of your stand mixer fitted with the whisk attachment, combine the flour, sugar, cocoa powder, baking soda, and salt and mix on low speed. Slowly add the oil and buttermilk. Increase the speed to medium-low. Add the eggs 1 at a time, mixing well after each addition and scraping down the sides and bottom of the bowl as needed. Slowly add the coffee, food coloring, vanilla extract, and vinegar. Mix the batter until just combined. Be careful not to overmix.

Evenly pour the batter into all 3 pans. Bake the 2 layers with graham cracker crusts for 27 to 32 minutes, or until a toothpick inserted into the center of a layer comes out just barely clean. Let the layers cool in the pans for 10 minutes, then invert onto wire racks. Let cool to room temperature. Lightly cover the layers with foil or plastic wrap so they do not dry out. Keep the oven on.

Bake the remaining layer without the graham cracker crust for 23 to 27 minutes, or until a toothpick inserted into the center of the layer comes out mostly clean. Let the layer cool for 10 minutes in the pan, then invert onto a wire rack. Let cool to room temperature. Lightly cover the layer with foil or plastic wrap so it does not dry out.

FOR THE MARSHMALLOW FLUFF

Clean your stand mixer bowl and whisk attachment and set nearby.

Bring some water to a simmer in the bottom of your double boiler. In the top, whisk together the egg whites, sugar, and corn syrup. Cook, whisking constantly, until the sugar is completely dissolved, about 3 to 4 minutes.

Remove the pot from the heat and add the vanilla extract.

Transfer the mixture to the bowl of your stand mixer and beat for 5 to 6 minutes on high speed, until stiff peaks form.

TO ASSEMBLE

Place a cake layer with the graham cracker crust on serving plate, crust-side up. Spread just the top of the layer with ¼ of the marshmallow fluff (please refer to the Basic Frosting Instructions on p. 18). Repeat with the second cake layer with the graham cracker crust and another ¼ of the marshmallow fluff. Top with the plain cake layer, bottom-side up, and spread the side and top of the cake with the remaining marshmallow fluff. If you have a butane torch, lightly brown the outside of the cake. Store in the refrigerator until ready to serve. Remove from the refrigerator and allow the cake to come to room temperature, about 20–30 minutes, before serving.

Grandbaby Notes: A double boiler is a two-story saucepan in which water simmers in the bottom to gently heat the ingredients in the top pan. If you don't have a double boiler, you can fill a pot with water and place it over medium-high heat. Then, place a heatproof bowl with your ingredients in it on top of the saucepan.

To make sure your egg whites will whip to stiff peaks, be careful when separating your eggs. Egg whites can be quite finicky, so the slightest amount of fat from the yolk can throw off the process.

André and me, Christmas 1983

Acknowledgments

I T TAKES A VILLAGE TO RAISE NOT ONLY A CHILD—IT TAKES A VILLAGE to raise a dream. When a lifelong dream comes true, you realize so many contributed to making it happen. This book was the biggest collaboration of my life, and far too many times the people who do the most work do not get recognized. From those who tested recipes, prayed for me, edited typos, selected the perfect cake plate as a prop, drove back and forth, purchased dozens of eggs when they were on sale, brainstormed ideas, or even talked me off the ledge when I screwed up a recipe for the third time after being up for 24-plus hours, I sincerely thank you.

First, thank you to God for giving me vision and persistence. None of this was remotely possible without You. To my loving mother, who is my best friend and role model, you made my dream yours, and I am eternally grateful for your belief in me. To my daddy, my hero, thank you for teaching me to dream big, aim high, and never settle. I hope I make you both proud. To my brother Alvin, thank you for your wild ideas that worked! We are kindred spirits. "Love is in your face." Auntie Rose, you are my other mother. Thank you for being my baking influence and warrior in the making of this book. Aunt Beverly, thank you for sharing your baking knowledge and love with me. I carry your torch with pride. Thank you Grand Mom Mom for your support as I go after my dreams.

To my long line of family who developed recipes, cooked, baked, passed down love, and created my family traditions, you are the reason why I'm here now. To all of my dear family; wonderful in-laws; Alpha Kappa Alpha Sorority, Inc, sorors; my dear friends and brainstorm team; my Blogger Boos; Inspiration Core and Visionary Nexus members; my Project Wedding ladies, my Infant Jesus, Marian Catholic, and fellow Clark Atlanta alum (A.Gunn-McNugget and Tisa-much love); Team Brightlight leadership; New Life Performance Company members; my former Columbia College, *EBONY*, The HistoryMakers, Judge Mathis, and Chicago Urban League crews; Fellowship "The Ship" members and New Faith members and my A Charitable Confection team, far too many to name, I love you and feel your support and prayers every day. I am on this path because of all of you. Thank you.

To my Uncle Sonny, A Mena, dear friend Leonore Draper, Tang, Anthony Hollins, and Mama Ramey, whom I know would have been my number-one taste testers, I felt your love and spirits in the kitchen. I miss you all so much every day!

To my godson Myles, I hope I make you proud and can be an example for you to follow your dreams with wild abandon. You can do anything you want!

To my agent Brandi, you believed in me from the very beginning and never quit making this dream a reality. Thank you! To my publisher, Agate, and to Doug, Danielle, Eileen, Kate, Zach, Jessica, and Morgan, thank you for the best partnership I could have ever imagined. Grandbaby Cakes found its perfect home in you. I appreciate all of the work you put into making this book so amazing! Thank you, Carla, for writing such a beautiful foreword to my very first book. You added the flavor, the love, and the spicy kick that pushed it over the edge of awesome. I'm grateful for your light and friendship.

To my creative team who worked tirelessly to make this vision come alive: my dear friend and prop stylist Leslie Watland, thank you for believing in me and making me start my blog in the first place! It was a pleasure creating this book side by side with you. And thank you, Jennifer Sauzer, for all of the rides back and forth! We appreciated you more than yellow cakes could ever say! Thank you, Jesse Szewczyk, for styling the loveliest cakes for this book. You were a blessing to our team and provided so much vision to this project. Thank you, Nicole Murphy, for your assistance in making this project happen! Thank you, Chuck Olu-Alabi, for capturing my family in the most beautiful way. They came alive in your portraits. Thank you, Courtney Waldon, for making the ladies of my family look oh so fabulous. To Sarah Little, you are such a rising star! To Lisa Bryant, Ava Smith, and the Smith family, thank you for sharing your beautiful talents with me! To the city of Chicago, thank you for the grant that supported the vision of this book. I am beyond grateful. Thank you, Snaidero Chicago, for the use of your beautiful space. Thank you, Pro Citrus Network, for the lovely lemons and limes you sent me to shoot with. It meant so much to this project. Special thanks to my management at the Lisa Ekus Group. Thank you, Lisa, Jaimee, and Sally for your guidance! Thank you, Sherri Maddick and Christina Isherwood, for believing in me and making me as visible as possible.

To my hard-working recipe testers, I am so grateful for the work you put into making these recipes work without fail. I could not have asked for a better group! Thank you Alice Choi, Allie Roomberg, Allie Hyshka, Amanda J.M. Vaughn, Amy Lee Scott, Amy Stachowiak, Brandy O'Neill, Deneen W. McBroom, Emily Paster, Monica Salas, Heather Imbraguglio, Jamila Lee-Johnson, Janelle Shank, Jehan Powell, Jennifer Eggleston, Jenny Bulllistron, Joan Hayes, Joanne Bruno, Joyce Delk, Kit Graham, Liz Harris, Marissa Evans, Mary Ann Graham, Melody R. Waller, Rose Ramey, Sara De Leeuw, The Food Temptress, Tiffani Belton, Tiffani L. Stewart, Wendi D. Rodgers, and Zainab Mansaray-Storms.

To my Grandbaby Cakes site followers and supporters, you are the reason why I bake with love and share every ounce of myself. You mean the world to me. To the food blogger community, thank you for embracing me.

And to my true love and husband, Frederick Adams, you are the true epitome of partnership. You are my dream catcher, voice of reason, imagination sidekick, creative partner in crime, ideation machine, and very best friend. We did it! Together!

And lastly, thank you to my grandparents, to whom I dedicate this book, Big Mama and Big Daddy. You taught me love through your example, and some of the best memories of my life were shared in your home. Today, my dreams honor you, and I will continue to acknowledge all you have been to me. Thank you.

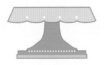

About the Author

Jocelyn Delk Adams is the founder of Grandbaby Cakes, a food website that is inspired by her grandmother and devoted to sharing classic desserts, savory recipes, and modern trends in an accessible way. Grandbaby Cakes has been featured in *Better Homes and Gardens*, *EBONY*, the *New York Times* online, *People* online, *Food52*, *The Kitchn*, *Fox News*, WCIU's *You & Me This Morning*, *Chicago Social*, the *Chicago Sun-Times*, and *SPLASH*, among many others. Jocelyn is also the founder of A Charitable Confection, an antiviolence dessert fund-raiser featuring the top bakeries in Chicago. Jocelyn hopes Grandbaby Cakes will inspire a new generation of dessert enthusiasts to learn to bake and not feel guilty about enjoying dessert.

Index